AF527403

Speaking plainly to The West

Abul Hasan Ali Nadwi

NADWI PRESS

NADWI PRESS

Nadwi Press Edition

Find our titles on your favourite online bookstore using the keyword 'Nadwi Press'

Originally Published by AIRP, Lucknow (India)
Reprinted by Nadwi Press in 2025

Translation of the Qur'ān

It should be perfectly clear that the Qur'ān is only authentic in its original language, Arabic. Since perfect translation of the Qur'ān is impossible, we have used the translation of the meaning of the Qur'ān throughout the book, as the result is only a crude meaning of the Arabic text.

Qur'ānic verses appear in speech marks proceeded by a reference to the Surah and verse number. Sayings (Hadith) of Prophet Muhammad (saw) appear in inverted commas along with reference to the Hadith Book and its Reporter.

Contents

Introduction

The fundamental problem of modern Islam is how to get Muslim society forge ahead with renewed vigour, power, and drive as a divinely guided society should and must. This question has exercised the minds of Muslims ever since the opening decades of the nineteenth century, when they found themselves enfeebled by decadence within and confronted with the growing might of the West striding forth in their lands in explosive restlessness. Their immediate reaction, and quite natural too, was that of a zealot who opposes the political and military expansion of his adversary with all his might and at all costs. The leaders of the Islamic East saw the West as something primarily to be rejected; they protested against its external encroachment as well as its corrupting influence their condemnation of everything western was deep yet narrow. They summoned the Muslim society back to its original purity and order; but having lost the capacity to order its life effectively, to refashion it morally, intellectually, and materially, the result achieved by them was not unexpected. Not only the East, including Muslim countries, passed into the political domination of the West, one after another, but it lost its self-confidence with the failure of its efforts.

On the other hand, the West launching forth with the greatest upsurge and expansive energy it had summoned up in its history, took the offensive from diverse directions-it was an unrelenting attack on a politically decadent and intellectually stagnant East from the directions of philosophy as well as culture.

The consolidation of political as well as intellectual superiority of the West produced another group of persons who, taking its superiority for granted, directed their protest solely against internal deterioration of the community. They advocated complete acceptance of the western mode of life and its way of thinking as the only way out to achieve political freedom; they wanted to carry the whole community as passive adherents along the tide of western liberalism that flowed around. They desired to harmonise the East with the West, but the harmonising sought by them was more passive and permissive rather than active and creative. They tried to redefine the content or the methods of faith in the light of western liberalism and some were even bold enough to declare that Islam would perish unless it did not come to terms with the modern world. The Shariah was considered by them as outmoded and inferior to the western legal system; they stigmatized the transcendental values of life as backward, medieval and reactionary. But their undue emphasis on worldly outlook succeeded only in producing apologetics for the external intrusion and menace, and a class struggle and schism in the community for still more decadence within.

However, both these groups those protesting against external encroachment and those condemning internal deterioration-failed to correctly estimate the real dimensions of the problem. None of them could adequately assess the ambitions, roots, and causes of the exuberant Europe nor could anyone generate a new synthesis of the East and West that might incite their people to constructing new dreams and adventures. If one failed to understand the secret springs of power wielded by the West, the other was carried away by its blind acceptance of everything western and modern. If one vehemently rejected the West; the other passively accepted it as an inevitable must; but none tried to meet it on terms of equality and mutual understanding.

In the lectures and essays included in this volume, the author points out to a third course. He reviews the situation in comprehensive terms in its true perspective and advocates that the vitality and skill of the West should be appropriated rather than accepted. He wants the East to be enlightened rather than to be intoxicated by the West. At the same time, he urges Muslim East to maintain its distinctive individuality, its faith, its moral integrity and the fervidness of heart and spirit; since, on its ability to do so depends on its capacity to play a useful role for itself, for the West and for the humanity at large. He focuses the attention on the fact, vividly clear yet overlooked by the critics as well as eulogizers of western civilization, that the modern West is moved by the philosophic vision of the ancient Greece which demands a complete separation of all institutions, customs, ideas, arts, and sciences from religion, rejects everything beyond the visible and the tangible and makes man a measure of all things. He brings out how these bases of Western thought and culture are antagonistic and incompatible with the values and ideals cherished by Islam as well as destructive to the West itself. Nevertheless, his thought-provoking criticism of the western intellectualism-its materialistic view of life, its failure in social and moral spheres and the resultant chaos threatening the entire world with moral and social disintegration- is neither destructive nor produced by an emotion of revengeful hatred of the West.

He underlines, on the one hand, the inner contradiction of the modern material progress-the contradiction of its astounding achievements in the physical field and failure on social, moral, and spiritual fronts-and, on the other, the capacity of the East to help the West out of its present predicament. He wants the

Muslim East to understand the real cause of material prosperity and worldly success of the West, accept only what is worthwhile, and, in return, help the West in overcoming its own follies and shortcomings, aberrations and excesses for their mutual benefit. He asks the East to guard and conserve its own latent energies of faith and righteousness, intellectual integrity and moral strength, and build a new bridge across which humanity may walk along to mutual understanding, progress and prosperity and material advancement as well as spiritual enrichment to create a brave new world-a world that would be worth living for all, for the white and the black, for the great and the small, for the powerful and the weak.

Lucknow:

May 10, 1973

Mohiuddin Ahmad

East and West

This lecture was delivered originally in Arabic on Friday, 11th October 1963, in the University of London. Translated by Dr. Zafar Is'haq Ansari, Lecturer, Petroleum University, Riyad, Saudi Arabia.

1

The well-known English poet Rudyard Kipling has said:

'East is East and West is West

And never the twain shall meet.'

Even though these are the words of a poet of our own century, the idea they embody has been a dominant one for many years both in the East and in the West, and has rooted itself deeply in their respective philosophies and literature. What has happened in this case is just what happens everywhere else: certain ideas and trends of thought emerge in a society, play their part in orienting its attitudes and predilections, and then comes forward a poet or a writer who expresses them in words of lasting beauty so that they gain currency and are referred to again and again by the people. This seems to have been exactly the case with Kipling's famous couplet: he epitomized the idea so long accepted in the East as well as the West, and in doing so emphasized even further the East-West dictum. I would even venture to say that I have not come across any literary or poetic expression which has caused so much harm to the good of humanity and to the concept of the unity of mankind as this idea of a perpetual division of the human family into East and West. No matter how simple and seemingly Innocent Kipling's words may be, nor how accurately they may describe an historical situation, expressions such as this have gone a long way towards leading people all over the world to regard the East and the West as two hostile entities which can never be reconciled. If East and the West were to meet, it could be only on the battlefield, and if they were to come together anywhere else, it would only be for mutual abuse.

This is what the East and West have felt for many centuries. They have remained apart, either in complete ignorance of each other or else possessing only an extremely superficial knowledge, seeing only those aspects of their rival's life which reveal weakness and ugliness, rather than strength and beauty. Their mutual behaviour has been determined by doubt and suspicion, contempt, and scorn.

The first serious encounter between East and West took place during the Crusades. This encounter could not lead to an appreciation of each other's good qualities, nor to an understanding of each other's beliefs and ethical attitudes. This was due primarily to the blind hostility of the Crusaders, which made them believe indiscriminately all kinds of fantastic reports about the beliefs and practices of the Muslims. In fact, it was their readiness to believe all sorts of travesties of the truth, such as, for example, that the Muslims were pagan brutes, that had helped the instigators of the Crusades to lead Christian fighters to battle for the liberation of the Holy Land. It is understandable that the atmosphere in which these wars were fought inhibited the growth of mutual appreciation, not to mention the urge for any serious study of each other's religious and ethical concepts, and prevented each benefiting from the other's accomplishments and experiences. Nevertheless, the Crusades were not altogether useless, for they reduced, even if they did not bridge, the gulf between these two groups of nations and continents.

To refer to more recent times, an encounter between the East and the West took place during the 19th century. This was the time when the West, driven by political and economic considerations, began to spread its influence and authority over lands of the East. The West invaded the East with all it had its civilization and industries, its sciences, its culture, its scheme of state organization- the good as well as the bad. The East, which had been left behind by the fast-moving West in its march towards scientific and economic development and towards a more efficiently organized order of things, was dumbfounded by the onslaught from the West and naturally could not be expected to be in the right frame of mind to attempt any effective understanding of the West, or to benefit by its accomplishments.

Another factor which prevented any appreciation of the West, if I might be excused for saying so, was the fact that despite its many healthy aspects, the Western civilization was on the whole the result of a materialistic view of the world and contained more or less all that is characteristic of a civilization whose religious impulse has suffered atrophy. Still another factor standing in the way of the proper appreciation of the West was- and here again I ask your indulgence-the strong feeling among Westerners that they were masters of the East. This was coupled with a feeling of racial superiority which manifested itself in their individual behaviour as well as in general policies which were incompatible with human dignity and the spirit of democracy: those very ideas for which the Westerners were celebrated and for which they had struggled in their own lands.

Another phase of the impact of the West on the East was the development of an attitude of slavish surrender and abject subservience among the peoples of-the East. They began to cherish Western values and ideas, adore the modes and manifestations of Western life and Western civilization. There arose a trend of blind imitation of the West, which robbed the peoples of the East of their distinctive personality as well as of their self-respect. This aping of the West in all walks of life pushed the Easterners into the background, reducing them to the position of mere camp-followers. Consequently, the West could not look upon the East with any sense of equality and respect, much less of admiration and esteem; nor could it look to the East for inspiration or guidance or anything original or creative. Eventually, matters came to a pass where complete dissolution of the East threatened its fading away into the West.

More recently, the peoples of the East have been engulfed by the idea of nationalism. The Western nations had resorted to nationalism as a substitute for the erstwhile bond of the Roman Church and for the religious sentiments which in the past used to arouse their enthusiasm. It may be pertinent, even though rather parenthetical, to remark that the West itself, having witnessed the disaster and destruction generated by narrow-minded nationalism, has endeavoured to extricate itself from this situation and is now well on the way to appreciating and admiring concepts of humanistic and universal import.

As for the East, the imported concept of nationalism seems to have taken root so deeply and engrossed it so overwhelmingly that despite the fact that once in the past it carried the torch of Divine Mission, it now dares not think once again of extending a helping hand to the West by giving it light and guidance.

More particularly astonishing and distressing is the case of the Muslims. Destined to be the custodians of the Divine Message in its perfect and final form, and entrusted with the task of leading humanity towards good, it is indeed a great calamity that they should have fallen prey to nationalism and become lost in its bye-ways, thereby narrowing down their spheres of interest and activity to limited geographical, racial or linguistic fields, and thus sealing to mankind as a whole the very source of those rays of light which would illumine all the world.

The emergence of Orientalism gave rise to many hopes. It was expected that the Orientalists would be able to bridge the gulf between East and West, and so bring about an understanding between these two branches of the human family and remove the barrier erected by ignorance and geographical remoteness. It was also hoped that they would be able to transmit to the Wet all that is best in the East in the way of prophetic teachings, moral values, examples of the noble life set by its prophets, and its spiritual leaders, the treasures of Eastern wisdom, and its wonderful code of laws and precepts for the guidance of human conduct.

There is no doubt that the Orientalists have many achievements to their credit. They resurrected many Islamic works which had for centuries lain buried from the light of day. They wrote a vast number of books which testify to their scholarly acumen. No one who has one iota of fairness and any love of learning can deny their academic approach and painstaking labours, their keen perception, and the scientific method of their work. The peoples of the East in general, and the Muslims in particular, nevertheless, feel that many of the Orientalists were inspired more by religious prejudices than by scientific motives. They have therefore disappointed the lovers of truth, who expected from them greater immunity from emotional predilections and inherited prejudices, a greater love for reality, a greater searching for the truth, and a greater courage in acknowledging it. However, Orientalism has failed, despite its virtues and accomplishments, to fill this gap, and could not give the West what the soul of many a Western man, disillusioned by the emptiness of a materialistic civilization, has been longing for, namely, a true and glowing picture of the religions of the East in general and of Islam in particular. I speak of Islam in particular because we Muslims believe it to be the last Heavenly Message- and therefore a message of everlasting value-to mankind, the message which bears the stamp of finality, which is in tune with the spirit of the age, which seeks to carry human civilization forward, and not, as some religions tend to do, backward; which is free from all extremism and rigidity, which is endowed with a wonderful capacity for creating new moulds consistent with the spirit of its own teachings as well as the demands of our changing times.

Whatever may have been the reasons, it is clear that the East, with its distinctive personality and its message, remained isolated from the West, and vice-versa. Whenever the two came together, it was in an atmosphere of suspicion and doubt, of bitterness and hatred. Seldom is there a meeting of minds between the East and West for the greater good of humanity and with a view to building an ideal civilization. And there is little readiness on the part of either to benefit from the other's characteristic capacities or to exchange skill and knowledge.

The East continued to work on its own ground, guid- ed by its own peculiar temperament which had been leavened by religion, inspired from time to time by noble prophets, and ceaselessly nourished by spiritual movements and the teachings of inspired religious leaders. The subject which interested the East was man himself, rather than that which is around man, or above his head, or beneath his feet. The East concentrated its attention and its intelligence, its genius and its willpower on man himself. It devoted itself to discovering the infinite secrets of man and plumbing the very depths of his nature. It devoted itself to arousing the capacities and powers that lie dormant within him; to orienting man's tendencies and inclinations; to refining and reforming his morals, without which human life can have no sound basis.

Those prophets of God-peace be on them all-came, and then in the end came the last of the Prophets, Muhammad. These prophets concerned themselves with man and his moral refinement, and opened up the treasures that lay within him, releasing therefrom light and life and knowledge, love and confidence, strength of purpose, contentment and happiness, and thus enabled him to discover the real source of all life and power and order in the Universe.

This also enabled him to view the Universe not as divided into numerous elements all warring with one another, but as a domain governed by One Omnipotent and Merciful Will. "His, verily, is all Creation and Commandment. Blessed be Allah, the Lord of the Worlds."[1] "The Lord of the East and of the West; there is no God save Him; so, choose thou Him alone for thy defender's"[2] the Quran says. Thus, the Prophets led to man's liberation from all forms of idolatry and dualism, from superstition and myth, from the authority of senseless tradition and legend, and from submission to all except the Creator and Ruler of the entire Universe.

Through this window opened by the prophets of God, man could also look at himself and his fellow men. It enabled him to see himself as the vicegerent of God in this world, as one in whom God had breathed a spark to His Divine Spirit, as one to whom He had entrusted a sacred mission, as one whom He had created in the best moulds, as one whom He had chosen for the greatest honours, as one whom He had invested with His deputyship, and upon whom He had placed the crown of government of this world; one for whom He had created all that is in the Universe, which He created for him and for His Own Self; before whom He had made the angels bow down low, forbidding him thereafter to prostrate himself before any other creature.

---

[1] Q. VII: 54

[2] Q. 73: 9

As God Himself says: "Surely We created man of the best stature,"[3] and: "We have honoured the sons of Adam; provided them with transport on land and sea; given them for sustenance things good and pure; and conferred on them special favours, above a great part of Our creation." [4]

Man looked through this window-the window opened by the Prophets and cast a glance at his fellow men, at the human family scattered throughout the length and breadth of the world. This enabled him to look at it as one single family, as if it were one soul, originating from the same parents. Men were seen as one brotherhood in the light of the Prophetic teachings, the worthiest of affection in the sight of God being he who was most benevolent towards God's family. This teaching also enabled man to feel that the members of the human race were the same as the parts of his own body, so that any feeling of pain in the one automatically caused plan to be felt in the other. It further enabled man to see that all distinctions between the various members of the human family based on colour, territory, or nationality, or on material possessions, is a legacy of ignorance: for man heard the noble Prophet say to his

---

[3] Q: XCV:4

[4] Q: 17: 70

Lord in the darkness of Night: "I bear witness that all creatures are brothers," and also heard him proclaim in broad Daylight, before huge crowds of people: "Oh men! All of you are from Adam, and Adam is from clay. There is no superiority for an Arab over a non-Arab; nor for a non-Arab over an Arab, nor for white over black, nor for black over white, except by virtue of piety." As God says: "Oh men, we have created you from a male and female, and made you into peoples and tribes in order that you may know one from another. Verily, the most honourable of you in the sight of God is the most pious among you."[5]

All the Prophets in their respective times and climes, and the Prophet Muhammad at the end of them all, strove to purify man. They mobilized to the utmost the Inherent capacities of man, which no branch of learning, neither philosophy nor psychology, could have ever accomplished. In fact, these branches of learning have not even been able to comprehend the dimensions of human capacities. The Prophets not only awakened and mobilized these capacities, but they also tried to organize and orient them for the good of the individual as well as for the good of mankind as a whole. The Prophets aroused in man an acute desire to seek God's

---

[5] Q. XLIX: 13

pleasure, to seek a relationship of intimacy with the Divine. They inspired man to love and obey God, and to love His creatures and serve them to ward off all unhappiness that might befall them, and to provide them with all that is conducive to their happiness and well-being, even at the cost of one's own self. The Prophetic teachings aroused in man the emotions of love, and graciousness, and delicacy of feeling and imagination. It gave man the ideals of purity of soul, nobility of conduct, greatness of spirit, and independence of worldly glamour, as well as sublimity of thought and aspiration.

These teachings created in man a longing for God, injected into him vigorous faith, and provided him with a knowledge of God, available from nowhere else. In short, man himself was the pivotal point of the activity of the Prophets, the ground in which they sowed noble seeds, and from which they reaped a rich harvest.

The Prophets of the East did not concern themselves with discovering, harnessing, and putting to use the forces found in the Universe, nor did they invent tools or machinery. Their attention remained focussed on inspiring man with good intentions, on creating in him a strong resolve to live well and do good. As for natural and industrial wealth, they obviously depend upon and are subservient to human will and direction.

Hence, whenever man is really well-meaning and has a will to serve some great cause, he manages to accomplish his objectives with the help of whatever tools are available to him at that particular place and at that particular time. Even if these tools are crude and of a primitive nature, the determination to achieve his goal makes them serviceable. In fact, if there is sincerity of purpose and earnestness, one can obtain greater achievements than can those who lack sincerity of purpose even though they possess tremendous resources. The reason for this is that when there is a strong and sincere will the unknown is somehow discovered, resources are made available, difficulties are overcome, and man makes a way for himself even over mountains and across seas. On the other hand, if there is no higher end in view or no determination to serve it the resources are wasted and the efforts of the inventors of the tools, and of the skilled labourers, are all brought to nothing. I do not wish to disparage the value of knowledge or of the instruments and machines invented by man to serve his ends. Nevertheless, I should like to stress that these are not so indispensable in comparison with some of the most elementary but strong urges of mankind. When, for example, a man is starving with hunger or dying with thirst or when love swells up in heart of a mother, or when a lover is overcome by longing, the intensity of the feeling itself impels them to find a way of satisfying and fulfilling it.

The role of the Prophets has been to place before man the right kind of objectives, and to fire him with the enthusiasm and devotion necessary to achieve them. Once this enthusiasm and devotion to goodness are present, men will find their own ways of self-fulfilment, even with the help of only limited resources and primitive tools, in the same way as a thirsty man or a mother burning with love for her child is driven to find the means of fulfilling that urge. It was this same intensity and sincerity of desire that led to the discovery of effective means of accomplishing those noble objectives which were given to mankind in their most perfect form by the last of the Holy Prophets. And those means were effective enough to bring forth a civilization that provided man with the utmost solace and comfort, honour, and dignity. Surely enough, this was of a comparatively simple pattern, devoid of all complications and complexities. And yet it contained powerful seeds and rich ground for good growth and expansion in the future.

As for the West, it began to wake up around the period of time known as the Age of the Renaissance. At that stage, due to a number of reasons the weakening of the bond of religious and moral values as a result of the misrepresentation of the Church, the pressure of economic and political factors, the struggle for life which the various European nations had encountered within the limited area of Europe, with all the problems arising therefrom-the attention of the West was turned from man himself to his external physical structure or to his environment; from the soul of man to the Universe, from the human heart to the physical world, and thus to sciences such as physics, chemistry, astronomy, mathematics, etc. And it is God's law that He gives to every man that for which he strives. As the Quran says: "Of the bounties of the Lord We bestow freely on all-on these as well as those the bounties of the Lord are not denied to anyone."[6]

The West began to make strides in natural sciences, discovering one secret of nature after another, achieving one success after another, till it reached its present level of attainment, undreamt of in the past. This needs no elaboration, particularly here in this place which is rightly considered as one of the pioneers of modern learning and Western civilization; and in this University, where I have the honour of addressing you, there has continued, as in so many other similar universities of Europe, the

---

[6] Q. 17: 20

advance of modern science and the discovery of the means for these astounding achievements in the fields of science and technology which are a blessing from God, the value of which should not be underrated. These resources were in the nature of a 'means', or an instrument. All this brought abundant wealth, tremendous power and energy and stunning speed, to such an extent that even considerably less than this would have sufficed for the well-being of mankind, for the establishment of world peace, for securing inner contentment and serenity and individual peace, for the spread of love and unity, and for mutual acquaintance and co-operation among the various branches of the human family scattered all over the globe. It could have removed the barriers that separate men from one another, so that they could extend the hand of co-operation and benevolence and sympathy to their fellow human beings in the remotest corners of the world; so that they could listen to the beating of their hearts and the whisperings of their souls, see their faces and hear their words, oppose the wrongdoer and help the wronged, feed the hungry and help those who are stricken. For all the preventive factors, which were the result of man's ignorance and weakness, and had plagued the life of man in the past, were gone. All kinds of instruments and machines were produced in order to help man to realize his objectives as quickly as possible, so as to leave no excuse whatsoever for any seeker after virtue, any lover of humanity and any standard-bearer of peace-neither individual, nor society, nor state.

These resources were enough to transform this world which is so full of wrongs and dangers and suffering into a paradise in which there would be no trouble, no fear, and no grief, no warfare and enmity, no poverty, and no disease. But was all that realized? Did we rid ourselves of fear and anxiety? Did poverty and misery end? Did wrong and tyranny cease to exist? Did peace and brotherhood prevail? Did confidence spread? Has the spectre of war been driven out of existence? I need not wait for your reply. For this great civilization has witnessed two great wars on a global scale and has shared the consequences and sufferings. All of us are living in the Atomic Age, and thinkers have virtually written libraries of books which portray the waywardness of this civilization, and the misery of the human beings who are subjected to it, pointing out the laxity of morals and the loosening of social bonds, the disintegration of the family, the growing mental tensions and anxieties, the predominance of fear and anxiety, as ominous developments in the life of modern man.

What has led to these results? The resources themselves were obviously innocent. The instruments and machines produced by modern civilisation were capable of being used for the good of mankind, for they have no will or direction of their own.

The answer to this is no secret, nor does it require extraordinary intelligence. The cause of all these misfortunes is that man himself has not been able to keep pace with the progress of the sciences. His intentions, tendencies and inclinations have not made the same progress as that made by instruments and machines. Indeed, it could be said that the sciences have progressed at the cost of man and his morals, at the cost of his soul and of his heart. The reason for this is that unfortunately the West has confined its activity and devoted all its intelligence and its willpower to the external world. The West concentrated all its efforts on the outer world, withdrawing its attention from man himself who is the very soul of this Universe and the masterpiece of creation. And even when it paid any heed to man's inner self, its approach was tainted by crass materialism which makes it impossible to plumb the depths of man's inner reality, to come to grips with the very solid facts of the inner life and appreciate faith and belief and morality. It also could not point out the source that guides man and inspires him towards goodness: his heart, upon the soundness of which rests the soundness of his whole life.

Unfortunately, even if the West wants to profit from the heart and guide humanity by it, it will not be capable of doing so, for it has lost the key which could open this lock. And however impressive the industries of the West may be, however fine their products, and however great the genius of the peoples of the West, they are incapable of opening or breaking the lock, for it is not the lock of banks and factories: It is a human lock, and the only key that can be applied to it is "faith". This key-the Key of Faith-which humanity obtained from the Prophets, has been lost, or lies burled amid the heavy burdens of modern civilisation or shambles of old religious centres.

The affliction of humanity lies in the separation of the West from the East, in the separation of knowledge from Faith, separation which has led to great disasters in the past. Faith had been making strides and growing for long ages in the East, while in more recent centuries, knowledge has been making strides and growing in the West. And Faith continues to wait for the companionship of science, while science stands waiting to submit itself to the guidance of Faith; and humanity is waiting for the two to come together and co-operate with each other in order to produce a new generation;

and there can be no hope of peace and true happiness without this blessed co-operation between Faith and Science.

As for the East, my friends of the West, its wealth does not consist of "oil", the black gold which you transport to your respective countries and then use it to run aeroplanes and automobiles. The real wealth of the East is that Faith which sprang up and blossomed there. You already benefited from some of this wealth at the beginning of your Christian Era. Then again in the opening decades of the seventh century A.D., the same treasure of wealth opened itself up again, in the forlorn desert of Arabia, and burst forth with a force and speed unprecedented in human history. Springing up from a remote valley in Mecca, it reached in no time to the farthest ends of the then known world, showering its blessings everywhere and refreshing, revitalizing, and enriching each and every nook and corner of the world, so much so that the entire earth blossomed forth with a new life. It can still be appropriated and made use of, if there are good intentions and creative boldness. It is still capable of overcoming all the problems confronting our modern civilization, and it can inject fresh vigour and vitality into our present civilization, giving it a new lease of life by providing it with a fresh sense of purpose and renewing its message, and reorienting the instruments and institutions of science and technology to worthwhile purposes. This can lead to momentous results, and to the creation of a new society in the best interests of mankind, the society for which the present age is yearning. Upon you, who belong to this great country, lies a great responsibility, for you were the pioneers of modern world civilization, and your national life is, even today, seething with energy and bubbling with vitality.

The Quran addresses you all, saying: "There hath come to you from God a new Light and a perspicuous Book-wherewith God guideth all who seek His pleasure to ways of peace and safety, and leadeth them out of darkness, by His Will into the Light, and guideth them to a path that is straight."[7]

---

[7] Q. V: 15-16

Islam the only way

Speech delivered at the Engineering University of BERLIN (West Germany) on Saturday the 14th of October 1964. Translated by late Sheikh Zahurul- Hasan, I. A. S., ex-Secretary, Revenue Department, Government of Uttar Pradesh.

2

It is the first occasion on which I have the privilege of addressing the mighty German nation to convey to them the message of Islam in this great city of Berlin. I am fully conscious of the heavy responsibility that rests on my shoulders and the delicacy of the task that faces me.

For centuries the German nation has enjoyed the reputation of being remarkable for courage, spirit of adventure, sobriety of thought, pragmatism, and capacity to work untiringly. It was because of these inherent qualities that this nation has produced a number of outstanding personalities, eminent in stature, both moral and intellectual, whose achievements left deep imprints on Western society, its philosophy and way of life.

To illustrate the above, I will mention only three out of the galaxy of these eminent men, who in their spheres, have very profoundly influenced the head and heart of Europe, and each of whom is, in his own right, the founder of a distinctive school of thought. Out of these I will mention Martin Luther first. He directed his attention towards and applied his energies to the Holy

Book with a view to bringing about a reformation in the Church as it existed then. He passionately preached for the containment of the unbounded rights of, and the curtailment of the unfettered powers enjoyed by the Pope and the priests. He left an indelible mark on Christianity and is rightly known as the founder of a religion: Protestantism. The next personality I wish to advert to is Kant, a profound thinker, whose 'Critique of Pure Reason' revealed the limitations of human reason and reduced the whole work of rationalists to a heap of ruins. And justly has he been described as God's greatest gift to his country. The third in my list is Nietzsche, an unorthodox and original thinker, who raised the banner of revolt against the prevalent ethical concepts and values, social system, and Christianity. He waged a life-long war against beliefs, fundamentals, and philosophies current in his time. Every one of these schools of thought or movements, whatever you prefer to call them, was remarkable for its courageous, revolutionising, and original way of thinking.

Dissatisfaction, restlessness and a desire for change. are the basic ingredients in the make-up of the German nation. The personality of Karl Marx embodied in itself revolutionary outlook and psychological restlessness at their highest level. Hence, he was able to infuse rest- lessness in a very large part of the world, a restlessness which is considered the greatest rebellion against the existing but archaic systems of the present age.

All the above mentioned movements were revolutionary in the real sense of the word. It may be that at times their spheres were limited, but often their fields of influence were extensive and far-flung; so was the case with their repercussions quite definite and deep at times, if light at others. Germans have always been distinguished for their bravery and boldness, their courage and progressive outlook, their Intense urge to attain a leading place among the nations of the world, and for their self- confidence. Even the last two World Wars were, in their essence, two revolutionary adventures in the sphere of world politics and domination. These adventures became necessary because of the sudden effervescence of enthusiasm and ambition which occurred in this Great Nation, bringing to the surface its capabilities and latent powers and thus created in it stout-heartedness and self-confidence. Even today this nation is fired with optimistic attitude towards life and its happiness and is fully conscious of her immense capacity for creative work, development and extraction of joy from life. But for these natural gifts, Germany could not have survived the catastrophes which have befallen her during the last fifty years and of which there are few parallels in history. It could not have withstood the two disasters each of which was enough to paralyse and overwhelm any other nation, and to sink it in the trough of despondency. Nor could it have arisen, Phoenix-like, from the ashes and debris created by World War II, to resume the struggle with renewed effort and vigour, to reconstruct its social, industrial and aesthetic life.

However, neither the adventures and experiences of this mighty nation, nor the revolutionary movements initiated by it could bring notable changes except within limited circles. This nation has undeniably played an important part in the orientation of European way of thinking and the evolution of Western society and has thus earned a deserved greatness and fame. It could not, however, totally transform the basic religious trends in Europe, nor could it repair the common man's way of thinking or renovate his mode of life. It failed to set up a new and healthy society or to create a new and better world. The two World Wars were fought for mundane objectives and not for the sake of purification of Christianity, nor for evolution of high moral values, nor for the establishment of principles of humanism, neither their objective was the wresting of leadership from the tyrant and unrighteous and to vest it in the just and merciful. They were not waged to stamp out sin, vice, lewdness, and inhumanity. I may be excused, if I say that they were in fact fought for the sole purpose of wresting power and supremacy. Both the contestants seemed to agree that injustice, tyranny, aggression, and spoliation may continue undisturbed but exclusively under its own supervision and guidance. With their high position and greatness in the comity of nations, the Germans could bring about a world revolution, more extensive and more far-reaching in its effect than that which has been achieved by all the past turmoil; a revolution which would have benefited not only Germany or Europe but the entire mankind, giving to the world genuine peace and contentment; a revolution more valuable because of its character, originality of concept, capacity to bring about a healthy change and creativeness. Such a revolution would have been far more valuable than any other brought about in the distant or near past by the distinguished and stout-hearted leaders of Germany.

Germany in spite of its setbacks is fully abreast with the rest of Europe, and it often appears to be ahead of it, in industries, craftsmanship and productivity. With its resources, inventions, productions and amenities of life, it is constantly forging ahead of most nations. But in the present order of things her role is limited to these fields only a role in which it has exhibited to a remarkable degree its intelligence and genius, its technical skill and perfection, its sense of discipline and perseverance. In these fields it has outdistanced many of her neighbours and occupies a leading place in the centres of international trade and commerce.

It was expected of this country which has always imbued with a spirit of restlessness, and which has ever been a cradle and home of revolutionaries, that it would rebel against a civilization which has converted man into a mighty wayward and destructive being, a civilization which has transformed man into a machine, deaf and blind, possessing neither soul nor heart, neither belief nor conscience. In this civilization the entire world has become a gambling den and an abattoir for souls. It recognises nothing as its objective except trade and commerce and has thus rendered life void of its real joy, variety, depth, and warmth. German nation was expected to rebel against the civilization in which life is nothing but an endless journey bristling with insoluble problems, an unending race, a fruitless effort, and aimless activity. Man, today is no better than a blindfolded bullock, tethered to an indigenous oil press moving endlessly round the axis of the machine. He has been deprived of his most precious asset, his noblest attributes-faith, conviction and sincerity and purity of thought and warmth of feeling.

It was no idle expectation that some European nation or other would rise in revolt against these base ideologies and artificial values, which, in spite of being man-made, are deeply cherished and which have imposed upon mankind certain standards of life and modes of living without any rhyme or reason, but are so taxing in their demands as to overwhelm a peace-loving man depriving him of his real freedom. German nation, the true worth of which had never been rightly appreciated by Europe, was particularly expected to bring about a change in the course of affairs; not only in its own land but throughout the whole world, and thus to open a new chapter in world history.

On the other hand, this consistently steadfast member of the family of European nations, though always envied, distrusted and unequally treated by them, continued to tread the same ideologies, and to co-operate with them for the achievement of the same goal- materialism- with all its kaleidoscopic genius and phenomenal efficiency. It made no attempt to overstep the limits it had set for itself, nor did it take the great leap forward which could at once change its destiny as well as that of the rest of the world; and in addition could secure for it world leadership, an immortal and elevated place in the ranks of nations of the world and an added respect for itself among her neighbours. No other nation but Germans could take this bold step a step which no other nation of Europe was capable of taking and one which would have broken the artificial and narrow boundaries within which Europe had been living for centuries, and after obliterating the old as well as the new, the oriental as well as occidental ways of life or thinking, would have rescued the world from the tragic results of materialism and tyranny science has brought so close to humanity. As compared to this, the achievements of all the revolutionaries and leaders in the field of Economics, Sociology, and Politics in the different parts of the world would have paled into insignificance.

It is a strange and incomprehensible paradox that Europe which is vigorously pulsating with life and replete with its good things, which leads the bulk of the civilized world, which has unmasked the Universe, harnessed matter and energy to its service and is literally a stranger to a static and inactive life is guided by a religious system, which, though it preaches humanism, believes in the existence of an intermediary between man and his Creator, and according to which, in the Crucifixtion of Christ lay the salvation of the entire human race, and thus subscribes to the principle of Vicarious Atonement, a dogma which by belittling the values of action and effort and their necessity ultimately leads man to depend upon others and whittles down his will and activity, initiative and capability. To cap it all, the representatives of this religion acted for a long time as barriers between the inquisitive, ambitious, dynamic people of Europe and the realms of knowledge and reason. Deviations from the theories advanced by the commentators of the Bible and from the teachings of the clergy, were considered heretical. Persons who in the light of their own commonsense, observations and experience gave vent to their opinion in any way different from those of the said commentators or the clergy were persecuted so cruelly as to remain unparalleled in the history of any other religion.

In course of time Europe rose against bigotry, narrow- mindedness and folly of, and the uncalled-for persecutions by the Church and broke all chains and shackles which had made it a captive and thus advanced materialistically to an extent unknown in history. Great strides were made in the field of civilization, literature, and social sciences. The efforts, unnecessary in quite a few cases, exhausted Europe mentally and physically. She lost that balance which is the mainspring of the genuine well-being of man and imposed upon her that extremism in attitude and materialism in outlook which, with the passage of time has become her ethos and second nature. The Church has even today a sway over many a Western country and by and large a European's attitude towards religion is divorced from all reason and commonsense, yet in matters relating to civilization and culture he acts quite independently of it. This contradiction between belief and action is the essential feature of every step which he takes towards progress and of every facet of his way of living.

Apart from this contradiction, the fact that Europe remained a stranger to Islam, a religion with unadulterated monotheism as its basis and having clear-cut beliefs, distinguished for its limpidity, practicability, dynamism, self- confidence, and respect for human endeavour, has been an event of tragic significance, the poignancy of which history can never forget. in the scale of values of this religious system, individual's effort and action occupy a very high place, so much so, that according to its cardinal articles of Faith, they are the basis of reward or retribution, both in this life and the Hereafter. According to it life is but a bridge to cross over to the next world; thus, inducing a man to develop the qualities of manliness, high-thinking, and noble-mindedness. Europe remained oblivious to the Apostle of this divine message about whom the Quran in its inimitable and majestic style, has said that he is "the Prophet who can neither read nor write, whom they will find described in 'Torah and the Gospel' (which are) with them. He will enjoin on them that which is right and forbid them that which is wrong. He will make lawful for them all the good things and prohibit for them only the foul, and he will relieve them of their burden and the fetters that they used to wear."[8]

Crusaders in their wake, the clergy and the missionaries and those European authors who neither had a bent for research nor possessed religious values, were mainly responsible for keeping Europe estranged from and antagonistic to Islam and its Prophet. They have presented both the Prophet and his Message in shockingly hideous colours as a result of which astonishingly false and baseless talks have gained currency about them. The dark hallows created round them by such stories, proverbs, and sayings, assiduously propagated for generations, prevented Europe from paying her tribute of love for them and acknowledging their greatness. Instances of such malignation can be easily picked out from any book written on them or cognate subjects during the Middle Ages or even long afterwards. Even today many a zealous Western author refers to and repeats these accusations, though with novel techniques and from new angles.

---

[8] Q. VII: 157

There has been yet another important reason for this antagonism. Europe saw Islam mainly through the Turks. Whenever there was occasion for Europe to ponder over Islam, the Ottomans were before her as Its accredited and sole representatives on the continent. She did not look at Islam from a detached, Independent, and objective point of view. To her it was the religion professed by the Ottoman Turks, who often attacked the Continent and occupied large slices of her land. They undoubtedly committed some mistakes and on occasions behaved unjustly and violently. All these blurred the vision and acted as hindrances in the way of the making of a balanced and sane appraisement of Islam. Such an appraisement, needless to say, could only be made by direct and unbiased study of the subject.

Europe's estrangement from Islam has had a very deep and far-reaching effect on the pace of history and civilization and on the development of human society. Had Europe or any of her important nations accepted Islam and sponsored its message, not only the Continent but the entire world would have been quite different from what it is today; life would not have been so utterly meaningless, nor would have religion and morality been so helpless and ineffective as they are today. Civilization would not have been speeding headlong towards destruction, and the East would not have been, as it is today, a free field for extermination, exploitation, extortion and oppression.

The world suffers from a void which has remained unfilled for centuries, a void caused by the absence of a nation strong in every respect-faith, morals and dealings, believing in and propagating the true and final divine message and thus facing the problems of the world boldly, leading humanity to its rightful destiny. Such a nation is required to be outstanding in current culture, genius, creative capacity, to be replete with energy and happiness, and to be a personification of action and effort. A nation with these qualities alone can divert the world from evil to virtue, from destructiveness to construction and from chaos to order.

The Turks led by the House of Ottomans could fill up this void in world leadership. Indeed, they performed this function in the East in the fifteenth century. They led the then Islamic world infusing into it a new life, impulse and energy. They could not, however, play this role in Europe mainly because of their backwardness in the spheres of modern sciences, organisation, invention, and genuine progress, as well as their continuous preoccupation with the task of repelling invasions of European nations, involving them in an endless series of wars. They could not lead Europe during Renaissance which gave birth to a new order. As a result of the above-mentioned factors, the Turks were outstripped by other nations of Europe and the vacuum is still waiting to be filled up by a nation, oriental or occidental, which may combine in itself faith and knowledge, insight into the potentialities of soul force and matter and integrate the eternal heavenly message, its all-pervading truth, with reason, knowledge and progressive outlook, the plethora of modern resources with holy objectives and thus attain the results vouched by the heavenly religions of which Islam is the last and the most perfect representative. Only such a nation can be the real leader and guide of the world, and fill up the vacuum; It alone can change the course of history, command the world to move in a new channel and forge a new path by bestowing upon the despondent humanity, bent upon committing hara-kiri a new lease of life, and thus pull It away from the very brink of the abyss of death towards which It Is inexorably head- Ing fast with rocket-like speed.

This would call for a daring revolution, a revolution before which all others brought about by the great revolutionaries and leaders of freedom and progress in the world turn Insignificant. It calls for revolutionary change in the attitude of the entire nation, a perilous leap involving tremendous sacrifice, from one way of life to another, from one order of things to a new order and from one faith to another. This vital step can bring to you, people of Germany, a leadership and a greatness, a respect and an influence, an importance and might, a sense of satisfaction and peace, spiritual solace and joy not even dreamt of by your intrepid, bold and war-loving leaders who plunged you into the fires of two horrible wars.

This leap alone can, by giving the right direction to your material power and political supremacy, make you the real leader of and the example for humanity as promised by Allah in the following verses of the Holy Quran: -

> "And We wished to be Gracious to those who were being depressed in the land, to make them leaders (in Faith) and make them heirs."[9]

> "And we appointed from among them leaders, giving Guidance under Our Command, so long as they persevered with patience and continued to have faith in our signs."[10]

---

[9] Q: 28: 5

[10] Q: 32: 24

Political freedom or cultural serfdom

Speech delivered before a well-attended meeting of students belonging to Indo- Pak sub-continent held in the Union Hall of the Leeds University, England on the night of Thursday, the 26th of June, 1969. It has been rendered into English by Mohiuddin Ahmad.

3

I feel happy to have this opportunity of speaking to you in your accredited University. A student like me having certain convictions would welcome such an occasion to convey his ideas to his friends this may not be an occasion of any special importance to you but for me it is quite significant for it affords me an opportunity to put in a word to such a select gathering of educated young men whom I hold near and dear to me.

You are fully aware that Europe came into contact with our eastern lands in the beginning of nineteenth century. Emerging from the nightmare of Dark Ages, Europe was only then enabled to reach out to the East. When Europe got the opportunity to chart its destiny after shaking off the gloom of medieval ignorance, it cast its glance towards the East. By that time certain Western powers had made some inroads into certain possessions of the Turks, but these were of minor significance. The real impact of the western civilization was felt only after a great western power gained a hold upon India and Egypt. India, Egypt and Turkey were then the three countries which, for varied reasons, occupied an important place not only in the

Islamic East but also in the entire world during the medieval ages.

India, then, occupied the pride of place. It was populated by a large number of Muslims who had wielded the sceptre of authority in that country with an unparalleled pomp and glory for several hundred years. They had enriched different branches of Islamic learning and, through their intelligence and industry, made a mark in the intellectual, cultural, social, and political fields in that country. When the British Government took over the control of India from the East India Company after the upheaval of 1857, it was thought that India would now ever remain under the suzerainty of the British Crown.

Egypt was of consequence because of its being the intellectual centre of the Arab World. It had the great Azhar University and the scholars, theologians, poets, and writers whose creations were highly admired all over the Islamic world.

I need not dwell upon the importance of Turkey in any detail. Being the centre of Caliphate, it was the home of a capable, gallant, and energetic nation which had played a crucial role in the history of the world. For all the three countries the contact with the West was not only a novel experience but it also gave a new direction to the course of history. It was their good fortune or ill-luck, or perhaps both, that all the three countries came within the sphere of British political influence at almost the same time. India was placed directly under the control of the British Government; Egypt became a protectorate where a British Political Agent was foisted under the garb of facilitating repayment of the loans advanced to that country; Turkey was undoubtedly able to save herself from the domination of the West, but it fell a victim to the political machinations of the Britishers. It can thus be claimed that the East crossed its path with the West through the country where we are present today. The historians now acknowledge that the injury first sustained by the East was at the hands of this very country. The East also came to realise its economic backwardness as well as political and military weakness by falling across the nation inhabiting this island. This happened in the beginning of the middle of the nineteenth century. Thereafter, as you all know, a tidal wave of national liberation emancipated, in quick succession, country after country from the political domination of the West. I attach more importance to the freedom of India if only because most of us belong to that sub- continent. The era of foreign domination has now come to an end. It had anyhow to wear away for it was unnatural. Of a fact, it was queerly anomalous that one country should continue to rule over a vast tract of another fertile and populous land, from across the seven seas and against the will of the nation inhabiting that country. It was an unusual phenomenon which lacked the capacity to support itself. Had it persisted for some time more, it would have anyhow run out its course by now. Viewed in this light, the Britishers have proved themselves to be more realistic than the French, for they were able to see the writing on the wall and to give freedom to their subject nations.

All these countries have attained independence from the foreign yoke; both India and Pakistan are now tasting the fruits of freedom, but they have still not shaken off the intellectual and cultural, moral and mental serfdom of the western civilization. Those of you who would have pondered over the present state of affairs would have surely noticed that after the attainment of freedom the shackles of intellectual bondage to the West have rather been strengthened. What were the causes for this development? An attempt to go into these would require a lengthy discussion. Varied reasons have been given by different writers and I have also discussed the question in one of my books on the subject.[11] However,

---

11 Western Civilization-Islam and Muslims published by the Academy of Islamic Research and Publications.

there is no denying the fact that all those countries which are attaining freedom from the political domination of the West are falling into a greater intellectual and cultural thraldom of western civilization. Now, you can yourself decide which of the two-the political freedom or the intellectual and cultural emancipation- was more significant. I do not hold a brief for political bondage of any country, for no freedom loving man can ever think of it. I would even assert that not a single self-respecting man would ever defend foreign domination or try to justify it. If there was ever a man who did so, he would have been prompted by his slavish mentality and immature understanding, but this is something Inconceivable to me.

But, I am constrained to refer to the fact a fact both regrettable and unpalatable-that none of our eastern countries including India and Pakistan and even those Arab countries which have yet to achieve complete freedom from foreign domination, has as yet realised what it really means to be independent and free. They have not yet enjoyed the fruits of real freedom. From the day they became free they have yielded themselves to be bound by fetters of intellectual, cultural and economic bondage. They have become so dependent on the West that the liberation of these countries has meant only a change in the personnel administering these countries without any change in the springhead supplying the vital impulse to run their administration. Liberation of these countries has not meant a whit more than this superficial changeover. We have been drawing upon the West not only in education but also imitating their system of education; we are aping the West in our manners and modes of living; and what is more, we often depend for our moral and religious precepts too on the researches made by the western scholars. Even the Islamic sciences are judged from the standpoint evolved by the western educational institutions. Orientalists are held in high esteem not only in West but in the East also and it has been accepted on all hands that whatever they say is the last word requiring no further quest and scrutiny. This is the present state of affairs in every Islamic country with the result that none of them has had an opportunity to enjoy the benefits conferred by their political freedom. All of them are so overburdened with the western ideals and view of life that they are seething with discontent beneath the insufferable weight of alien crazy concepts. Some of these countries are, fortunately, wholly populated by the Muslims, but they have failed to pattern their polity on those principles and traditions of Islam which are the demand of its faith and conscience. They are, in consequence, caught in the cobweb of mental discontent and vexation of spirit which is bound to result into a crisis of confidence and disintegrating conflict.

An unrelenting struggle in these countries is caused by those who wield the reins of Government in these countries, those who have pinned their faith in the western ideals and concepts. They are Muslims, no doubt, and they also come from respectable Muslim families. Nor have they forsaken Islam, but in their mental make-up and intellectual outlook they have been cast in the mould of western way of looking at things. It is their misfortune that the nations committed to their care are Muslims out and out; they have faith in God and His Apostle; they believe in the life after death where there is a heaven and a hell and where they shall have to render account for whatever they do in this world; they acknowledge the fact that the life of the world and its pleasures and sorrows are transitory; they are convinced that the ultimate end they have in view is preferable to the purely material objectives; they know that the aim of life is not to eat, drink and be merry and to have the fat of the land but it consists in being more humane, inculcating the awe of God, be taking the path of virtue and avoiding the ways of sin, leading a life pure and virtuous in the footsteps of the last Prophet of God, acting on the injunctions and precepts of the Law revealed by the Lord, serving the humanity and disseminating the message of peace and virtuous living to the wayward humanity in order to help it to chart its course out of the predicament of doom and despair it is finding itself enwrapped at present.

But those who have gained a hold over administration in these countries have an entirely different view of life and the world. They harbour doubts about many a truth enunciated by Islam. They are sceptical if there is any Power behind what their senses reveal to them-a Power unseen and imperceptible behind the manifest, palpable beings and objects or that there is a life after death. They find it hard to believe that man can derive satisfaction and happiness from anything other than material assets and holdings. An unprecedented but unfruitful unrest has thus cropped up in our eastern countries, which is wasting their energy for nothing. Only yesterday I told some of my Arab friends that if our eastern countries could get a leadership which was aware of the inherent qualities and strength, the indomitable courage and enthusiasm, the spirit of zeal and sacrifice, the mood and temper and the glorious past and present potentialities of our people, it could again brace up their strength which no power on earth would be able to subdue.

Whatever vigour and energy the East possesses, it lies in the power of its Faith. It is the faith that moves mountains. For the people in the East, the faith still has the power to awaken the spirit to sacrifice their lives, their pleasures, their hearths, and homes for it. Fighting for the honour of God, for Islam, for the Prophet and for the faith still stimulates that frenzied fervour in them which can neither be enkindled by a call for any other cause nor be subdued by anyone.

But it is simply tragic that our people passing out of the portals of western universities have all their wits about them except that they remain completely oblivious of the latent strength and vigour of their own people. If you do not mind my plain speaking, I would say that perhaps the Poet of the East had addressed these very persons in this couplet.

Get within thyself and discover the life's secret; If thou does not want to be mine, true to thyself be at least.

All those who go back from the universities here know all about history and geography, individual and mass psychology, but if they remain blind to anything, it is the temperament and disposition of their own people -the people amongst whom they have to go back and live and work, the people who are their own limbs and hands. They do not know them, nor the reservoir of strength concealed in them which had once shaken up the world. It is the power that can never be defeated even by the combined strength of all the nations of the world. And our people in the East have that power of faith even today but either our leaders know not what it is or they are strangers to the parlance of faith. They perhaps only know the language which reaches the ears of their people but fails to touch their hearts. They cannot speak in the tongue that can enrapture and enravish their hearts-a language that touches the cords of one's heart and casts a magic spell on the listener. This is the language of the faith and the Quran; the language spoken by the companions of the Prophet which made men die in the last ditch. How can a man speak to others unless he knows their language? How can I convey my thoughts to the people of this land unless I can speak in English? This will lead to nothing but to the confusion of tongues.

These leaders speak to their own peoples in the same parlance in which they converse with the West. They should have at least been alive to the fact that the people whom they seek to accost are the followers of the Prophet of Islam. The language which they understand, which touches their heart and stirs their blood is the language of faith-the language that they speak in their homes and lanes, mosques, and marts. It is the language of those transcendental realities which they have cherished for fourteen hundred years. Therefore, if you want to tug their heart stings you shall have to speak to them in that very language.

I do not mean to oppose the cultivation of modern sciences. You should try to learn as much of these arts and sciences as possible. I would rather congratulate you and your guardians for sending you here to glean the knowledge of the West: you should rather try to make yourselves masters of these sciences, learn all about them and undertake original research in these branches of learning. This is the greatest need of the time.

But, my dear friends, there is a vast difference between the means and the end. I have this walking stick in my hand. It gives me support when I walk; it can even be helpful in defending myself. But it can never take the place of any objective I aspire to achieve. If I can get a better stick or if I am enabled to give it up, I shall at once throw it away. There was a time when it was the only weapon possessed by man but as he learnt to manufacture better weapons, he abandoned it.

There is nothing like old and new, modern and ancient in human knowledge. I have never accepted this view, for knowledge remains ever fresh and new. Whatever you call the ancient branches of learning were once the newest ones, and whatever is known to be modern today might become old and stale after fifty years. The scholars might then feel ashamed of subscribing to the views held today. All this quibbling about old and new is meaningless. You should gain mastery in all the languages, arts and sciences in chemistry and engineering, in history and fine arts, in philosophy and psychology, but you should treat them only as means for achieving a higher end.

The disintegrative forces consuming the eastern countries are the result of unnecessary embroilment which is wasting their energy. The cause lying at the root of this strife and dissension is that our leaders, although physically present in the East, have their minds and hearts in the West. The nations with whom they have to pull on, live and die amongst whom are staunch believers. They can be summoned up to stem the tide only as Muslims.

You are not the off springs of any primitive tribe inhabiting the Dark Continent which has found itself suddenly amidst the civilized nations of the world. I do not mean to denigrate the people living in the Central Africa who have just come across the civilized world. There are still cannibals in the world. Somebody told me recently that the first Christian missionary who went to

Fiji Islands was roasted and eaten up by the natives who then continued to sip the soup of his boots for consecration. But you are not the progeny of a savage tribe without any history, civilization, or faith, nor do you belong to a nation that has suddenly made its debut from darkness to light, which has been overwhelmed by the technological progress of the West, and which is staring open-mouthed at the wonders of electricity and aeroplanes, the populous city of London and its multi-storied buildings. Believe me you are not the sons of any nomadic clan or a wild tribe.

You are the progeny of a nation that had once guided the world and saved the sinking ship of humanity. I recently told my Arab friends that when the humanity was at the verge of destruction, it were they who were first to embrace Islam and to snatch the world from the jaws of death. Today, we are sailing with them in the same boat. Both of us have fundamental difference with the West. We ought also not to follow the West blindly; It was only because of our own shortcomings and the shortsightedness of our leaders that we have lagged behind the West in the field of education and learning. The West has now gone ahead of us. This was our misfortune, no doubt, but there is no denying the fact that it was we who showed the way of knowledge and progress to the world. The world was committed to our charge in the past and even today no other nation except ours, has the capability to conduct the ship of humanity to the shores of safety. You have witnessed how the West has managed the affairs of the world. It has, undoubtedly, filled the world with novel inventions and achieved what was considered beyond the bounds of possibility. Some time back a European scientist proudly told an Indian philosopher that the West has manufactured such fast-moving aircrafts which can cover the Atlantic Ocean in a few hours. He went on with his detailed narration of the achievements of the West. The Indian philosopher patiently listened to his tall talk and then replied: "Yes, you have learnt to fly in the sky Ilke the birds and to swim in the oceans like fishes, but you have still not learnt how to walk on the earth like human beings." The reply of the Indian philosopher epitomises the achievements of the western nations. They have great achievements to their credit, but they are still groping in the dark about their ultimate objective.

The first and foremost thing one ought to know is the reality of man. What is the ultimate end of human life, and what should man do to achieve that objective? The West has no light to shed on these fundamental questions., and that is why all the achievements of the western nations have been turned into child's play. The fact is that the western civilization is enacting a drama. You would have seen many dramatic performances and enjoyed them too. So is humanity enjoying today the performances of space travels and seafaring skills. But what is the end result? How much humane has man become? What progress has he made in spreading humanitarianism? How much have men come nearer to each other; have the feelings of love and compassion Increased or decreased; have they learnt to keep peace with all men; how much has man become enlightened in mind and heart; has he achieved peace and solace of heart; has he discovered his ultimate goal; have his moral qualities enhanced or abated; has he eschewed cruelty, lewdness, ruthlessness, and learnt not to take delight in subduing others, robbing and plundering other people and humiliating his fellow beings? Has the realisation dawned on him that so far, he has been treating this world-as Iqbal has aptly described as a "gamblers' den" that has taken the humanity through the holocaust of two world wars? Tell me honestly what has been the result of this technological progress? What man has gained by it? I want to know how far has our progress helped the humanity to march ahead on the path of peace and prosperity, how much peace of heart has it attained and how nearer has it come to its ultimate goal? We see today more injustice, more ill-will and more enmity in the comity of nations. Acts of flagrant injustice are being committed today in broad daylight. Take the instance of Palestine. The powerful nations of the world banished the inhabitants of that country to make it the national home of another people who had already been settled is other lands for thousands of years. All the appeals to equity and justice have failed to have any effect upon the conscience of the world. Would you still call it a civilized world? Has any big power-America, Russia, or England-the moral courage to acknowledge the injustice done to the Arabs? Are there even a few persons in this country who would courageously aver that the promises made by them to the Arabs were broken by their leaders? You would not find any other example of such wanton injustice and immorality in the entire history of mankind. This was not an unpardonable injustice to one nation alone but a crime against the entire humanity. The fact of the matter is that an uncanny drama of gross injustice is being staged against the whole human race, deadly weapons capable of destroying the world in a few seconds are being developed; and, animated by mutual jealousy and distrust the big nations are arraying themselves against each other which might result in the doom and destruction of all the nations of the world.

You are aware that America has plenty of such munitions of war which can destroy the world in a few minutes. Russia and China as well as Britain and France are also building up similar arsenals. They have already got massive missiles and aircrafts which can carry these explosives to the remotest corner of the earth. It seems that some heartless fellow has given knives and daggers to a few stupid children who are too willing to pounce upon one another and only God knows when one of them would deal a deathblow to others.

But you belong to the nations which have an ideal, a goal of life and a set of beliefs and convictions. Your people will never be content with the materialistic civilization of the West. Nevertheless, you may gain whatever knowledge you may get here but you should never accept the viewpoint of the West as the final word, nor regard the western nations as guardians of the world. It is not befitting of you to consider the nations of the East as uncivilized brutes for whose enlightenment and advancement the West has to play the role of a ministering angel. If anyone of you holds such views, then, believe me, there would be none more unjust than he to his own people and to his glorious past. You have thus to take only those things from the West which you cannot find in the East. Still, you should never lose sight of the fact that these people too lack certain things, and they have to learn them from you in the same way as you have come here to acquire the knowledge of certain arts and sciences from these people. It might be difficult for you to enumerate the things that the East and West have to learn from each other or to decide which of these are more important. I also do not propose, for the present, to dilate on this point, but it would suffice to add that the things you can teach them are of far greater consequence than those you can learn from them. For you can show them the way to lead a life of goodness and virtue which is as much essential for success in this world as in the next. But if you are unable to learn what the West can teach you, it would mean, at the most, a little delay in material progress, some inconvenience and a bit more effort for the East to catch up with the West. This explains the difference between the worth of what the West possesses, and the way of life chosen by your people in the East. And now you can decide which of the two is more worthy and valuable.

Dangerous self-conceit

Article written in 1949 and published in 'Daily Tameer' of Lucknow. Later on, rendered in Arabic to be published in 'Al-Muslimoon', of Damascus. Has been rendered into English by Mazharuddin.

4

It is related that a Rajah belonging to a high caste was very nearly drowned while taking bath, but a man of lowly origin who watched him in his plight ran to help him and brought him safe on the shore. When the Rajah recovered his consciousness, he asked the name of his benefactor, but when he was told that the man belonged to a low caste, his anger knew no bounds. He ordered that the man should be dealt with very severely for having defiled him by his unholy touch. Accordingly, the man was severely punished so that he might serve as an example to others.

It happened, perchance, that the Rajah found himself in the same plight a second time and, by a strange coincidence, the same man was standing at some distance from him. He could have easily saved the Rajah, but he remembered his punishment and merely looked on, with the result that the high and noble Rajah lost his life.

You might have already heard the story. You may think that it is an exaggeration. However, there is nothing strange in it, if you take into account the oddities of the human mind. Family pride and national self-conceit have drowned many individuals and peoples, bringing ruin and destruction upon them. Thousands of individuals and hundreds of nations have been so blinded and led astray by their prejudices and conceits that they preferred to go the way of annihilation and extinction rather than pay heed to the voice of those whom they regarded as their inferior, by force of tradition, or who had the misfortune not to belong to their own people. You will come across many examples of this in the moral and religious history of mankind. Recent history of the civilized and progressive nations of the world is not also entirely devoid of these examples. The history of the drowning self-conceited Rajah whose insane pride and folly you regret, is not some ancient story of very distant times or the fabrication of some learned mind. It is a real story of the oddities of the human mind recurring throughout history. The part of the hero has been assigned to a Rajah, but the tale represents a historical truth explaining one of the underlying causes of the death of nations and peoples.

Have you heard the name of Greece, where world famous philosophers, poets and scientists were born? Who does not know the names of Plato, Aristotle and Socrates? When you read the history of Greece, you feel that the country was literally a mine of genius and talent. Nature seemed to have been particularly generous to the people of Greece; it had endowed them with all the qualities and provided them with every material resource necessary to make a people great and prosperous. Philosophy, science, literature, poetry, mathematics, sculpture and architecture flourished with unmeasured abundance. Greece was the fountain-head of the creative arts that required human ingenuity and intellectual refinement. It was the leader of learning and enlightenment in the then known world and nations of the world prided themselves on being its disciples and followers. In spite of all this, however, there are things which do not come within the purview of human intellect and which no human ingenuity can discover or explain. These are the secrets of life, such as, how the physical world came into being, who created it and why and how long it is going to last; is there any other life after death, if there is one, how is it related to this one; and then there are questions such as what is evil and good, what is lawful and what is unlawful? Questions such as these cannot be answered by the unaided human intellect or by logical hair-splitting. The Greeks treated these problems as if they were problems of literature or poetry, but this was not the field of literature or poetry. The result was that the Greeks committed blunders at every step. They attributed to God frailties of which even human beings feel ashamed and which make the Divine Being powerless in relation to man's ethical and social conduct. They invented a whole hierarchy of Reason and Heaven without rhyme or reason and made the entire life of man depend upon them. They further rationalised the ancient Greek mythology and clothed with religious sanctity a whole host of gods and goddesses. The result was that the moral and religious life of the ancient Greece was emptied of all reality. The fear and love of God went out of the souls of men. The love stories of gods and goddesses filled the literature with abject sensuality and the religious environment became polluted with carnal lusts. The accepted standards of good and evil lost the sanctions behind them. Philosophy provided moral justification for every act of treachery, lust and sensuality. Men of learning came forward to support prostitution and explained the benefits to be derived therefrom. Thus, the proverbial land of philosophers and poets fell a prey to moral chaos, and the lamp of learning and light was finally extinguished by the gales of sexual immorality.

Just at the time when Greece was passing through its final stages of moral degeneration, there arose in the countries to the south-east of Greece, which were intellectually backward and scientifically lethargic, men who have been called the prophets. They were neither poets nor philosophers like the great men of Greece, neither were they learned in mathematics or arts. They were, however, men inspired with faith and armed with guidance. God had vouchsafed to them knowledge of His attributes, the secrets of life, and the certainty of the final human destiny in a life still to come. These people had in their possession the quintessence of all knowledge and reality. The Greeks had only a tangled web of knowledge, which became more and more difficult to unravel as the time passed. The Greeks were still playing with pebbles on the seashore of knowledge, while the prophets had fathomed its depths and crossed its currents bringing pearls of wisdom for the guidance of mankind. The Greeks knew everything except themselves; they had ranged across the frontiers of all human history and learnt all about the then known world; only they did not know about the Creator of the world and its Nourisher and Sustainer. The morals and philosophy of the Greece had lost all soul-force, and became entirely incapable of Inspiring a single human being with piety and purity: carnal lusts, intellectual anarchy, and moral chaos had taken deep roots in the soil of Greece. In contrast, the prophets of the East were a dynamic force; whomsoever they touched he became morally and spiritually purer and felt himself freed from the domination of desire. Their disciples and companions seemed to develop higher and holier motives as they came into contact with them. The philosophers of Greece could not, for all their learning and erudition, enable a single man to stand up against his desires and remain firm and persevering on the path of virtue. The prophets of the East, without so much as making an attempt to teach their followers anything by way of book learning, raised the latter to new and higher levels of morality and armed them with so much spiritual power that they could easily triumph over their lower selves.

These prophets offered their guidance to Greece without any request from her and without any demand for monetary reward, but Greece turned away with a scornful smile saying that it was an insult to her learning and intellect to accept the guidance of illiterate persons who were so utterly ignorant of her arts and sciences. The Greeks claimed that they were adepts in all sciences and need not turn to others for help. The result was that the sciences and arts of Greece on which she prided herself became millstones round her neck. Her civilization, devoid of godliness and lacking spiritual guidance was poisoned at its source; its strength was sapped and finally it tottered to its ruin. The Quran has given us a vivid description of the situation as it then existed: -

"For when their apostles

Came to them

With clear signs, they exulted

In such knowledge (and skill)

As they had; but

That very (wrath) at which

They were wont to scoff Hemmed them in."[12]

Exactly the same fate overtook Rome, which was the political and intellectual heir of Greece. It surpassed Greece in the external organisation of society, in the art of constitution-making, in political administration, and technical knowledge of warfare. Rome comprised within its iron grip all the three continents of Europe, Asia, and Africa and their far-flung colonies. In extensiveness of its conquests, the strength of its political edifice, the skill of its constitution-makers, and the development of its architecture, sculpture, and painting, Rome had no equal in its day of glory. But it also failed to discover the secrets of life, strength, and vitality, and to draw inspiration from the life-giving message of the prophets. It too

[12] Q. XL: 83

revelled in idolatry and worship of human gods, it too remained deprived of sound moral values and the correct guidance of divinely inspired personalities. The result was that, like Greece, it fell into the vortex of social and moral evils. Its life became burdened with extravagance, luxury, insensate pleasure-loving and economic exploitation of class by class, until it developed a cruel interest in gladiatorial sports, flagellation of slaves and excruciation of helpless men and women.

In this period of moral degeneration, there were born a great many prophets of God in the eastern possessions of Rome. The fame of their teachings spread to Rome, its cities and towns and Imperialist Rome refused to listen to their voice out of self-conceit, because they came, so the Romans thought, from subject lands under the dominion of Rome. The Romans believed that they were born rulers. How could they bring themselves to follow those whom they regarded their slaves! It has always been the stock argument of men in power that: -

"If (this Message) were

A good thing, (such men)

Would not have gone

To it first, before us."[13]

The Romans took no cognizance of the prophets and were speedily brought to ruin through their national self-conceit which produced among them the destructive evils of immorality, anarchy, and self-indulgence.

"That was because there

Came to them the apostles

With clear signs,

But they said:

"Shall (mere) human beings

Direct us?" So, they rejected

(The Message) and turned away

But God can do without (them), And God is

Free of all needs,

Worthy of all praise."[14]

---

13 Q. XLVI: 11

14 Q: XLIV: 6

In the sixth century A. D., Rome, Persia, China and India were the most civilized countries of the world, but the sense of human fellowship had become enfeebled everywhere. The lamps of guidance lit up by the great prophets burnt dimly and were on the point of extinction. Science and learning had become devoid of the inspiration of faith and of the true knowledge of God. Religion and culture were under the sway of superstition and in politics, social life and morality, human desires had full and unrestricted play. Both kingship and priesthood had been reduced to the worst kind of tyranny. Houses of worship had become centres of immorality. Christianity, Zoroastrianism and Hinduism all seemed to have lost their spiritual glow. These religions had become incapable of creating among the masses or the intellectuals any desire for moral purity, dutifulness and real piety and fear of God. They lacked clear-cut principles on the basis of which a healthy social or collective edifice could be raised. In Persia and Rome ever fresh taxes and fines made the life of the poor miserable and they became so completely absorbed in the cares and anxieties of everyday existence that they could give no thought to the deeper problems of life. The middle classes had been completely corrupted by the desire of more and more wealth and by an insatiable craving to model their lives after those of the richer classes Life had become so costly and living standards had risen so high that the Persian nobles gave away thousands of rupees to purchase a single headwear. In their dresses, diets and household adornments the Persians had gone to the last extremities of luxury and refinements. In India caste-divisions were becoming even more rigid and the natural differences between man and man were in- creased a thousand-fold by artificial distinctions. Sexual immorality invaded not only the literature of the land but also the temples and sacred houses of worship. Wealth and power became the sole objects of human endeavour. Religion was reduced to a few meaningless rituals and philosophic wranglings. In short, the civilized nations of the world lay prostrate under the benumbing weight of their own culture and had lost all capacity to receive and accept the Divine guidance.

God in his wisdom selected for the spiritual regeneration of humanity a people who, though they were idolatrous and no whit behind other nations in their immoralities, were yet free from the evils created by a highly artificial civilization and by the wealth and power of a far-flung imperialism. From among these people God chose a person distinguished by his noble heritage and noted for his extraordinary qualities of wisdom, courage, large-heartedness, and capacity for leadership.

He proved by the success of his missionary efforts, by his perseverance, hard work, and his moral purity and spiritual greatness that no man among the whole of mankind was better fitted to shoulder the immense burden of prophethood. Mankind had grown to maturity and the future of the world pointed clearly to the fact that it could no longer remain divided into racial and national compartments. Accordingly, Mohammad, the Prophet of God, gave to the world a social and religious order complete in its details, clear in its outlines and final in its conclusiveness that provides for the needs of all nations in the world, all classes among the nations, all individuals in the different classes and the circumstances of each individual's life and offers adequate guidance to the poor as well as the rich, the rulers as well as the ruled, the young as well as the old, the civilized as well as the uncivilized, the high intellectuals as well as the unlettered and uneducated masses of human beings. In the social-religious order of this society each individual is afforded opportunities of development to the utmost of his capacity and achieving the highest spiritual progress within human limits. No divisions of race, nationality and historical periods are admitted in this system of life which contains within itself metaphysical tenets as well as well-defined and clear-cut principles and laws for the regulation of human needs. These laws do not require amendments, additions and alterations. Moreover, the system of life brought by the Prophet Mohammad contains not only most important legal precepts and social laws, it provides adequate spiritual motives for the observance of those laws and principles and powerful psychological deterrents to restrain the people from disobedience and violation of those principles. And his teachings are backed by the highest force of personal example and a life of dynamic activity lived in accordance with them.

This socio-religious order of society was the common heritage of the entire humanity, each nation and each country having an equal interest therein. it gave equal chance to all peoples to achieve the maximum of progress. No nation or race had a monopoly of this socio-religious order; the Prophet himself had explained that "Each one of you is descended from Adam and Adam was made of clay. The Arabs have no superiority over the non-Arabs, nor the non-Arabs over Arabs, except on grounds of piety and moral purity. Men were divided into tribes and families that they may be distinguished from each other, the highest and most respectable in the sight of God is he who is most God-fearing." In the first period of Islam, we find Salman of Persia, Suhail of Rome and Bilal of Abyssinia and their several compatriots working side by side with the

Quraish of Mecca and the Ansars of Madina. We hear a great Caliph like Omar address Bilal, the Abyssinian, as "our chief and leader". Even later in the history of Islam we find neo-Muslims and Persians occupying the chairs of religious learning in the cities and centres of knowledge of the Islamic world offering religious guidance to the Arab chiefs and Muslims who had inherited Islam from their forefathers, and it is known for a fact that their verdicts commanded universal respect and obedience. Once Abdul Malik, a famous Omayyad Caliph, enquired of a traveller the names of the religious heads and distinguished men of learning in the great cities of Islam. He was surprised to learn that only in one city, the highest position among men of learning had gone to an Arab. In all other places non-Arab slaves or men descended from non-Arab slaves, occupied the highest seat of learning. On the occasion of Hajj, the greatest international gathering of Muslims, when the elite of the whole Muslim world come together at one place, it used to be announced that no one else except Italian Ribah a freed slave, was competent to deliver verdicts on disputed questions. The whole history of Islam furnishes ample evidence to show that Islam gave equal and unfettered opportunities of development to men of diverse nationalities and races who accepted its message and joined its ranks, and it elevated them without the slightest distinction of race or nationality and on this basis was fulfilled the prophecy of the Quran about the Prophet Mohammad in respect of the oppressed and down-trodden people. The Quran stated about the Prophet thus: -

"He urges them to do good and prohibits them from evil-doing. He makes clean things lawful unto them and makes unlawful unto them things which are unclean, and he removes from them the fetters and burdens which weigh them down."[15] They tasted the sweetness of life for the first time, and they achieved progress in all directions. Politically they founded kingdoms and empires, intellectually they added to the treasure-house of learning.

Islam spread to Europe through the doorway of Spain and flourished in that country for nearly eight hundred years. The Arabs of Spain suffered from many shortcomings. They were certainly far behind the companions of the Prophet in point of religious sincerity and missionary fervour, still Europe had splendid opportunity during the Arab rule over Spain to study the principles and laws of Islam through the writings of Spanish Muslims and examine its characteristics as a new

---

[15] Q. 7: 10

social order. But Europe missed this opportunity owing to its religious prejudices and racial pride, two peculiarities which have always marked it and which it has received from ancient Greece and Rome as its spiritual heritage. The people of Europe always looked upon Spanish Muslims as their political enemies. They did learn science and philosophy from Spanish Muslims but took no notice of what was really valuable in their social life, until at last in a frenzy of religious prejudice and blind hostility they drove the Muslims out of Spain towards the African continent and then set out to efface, in a spirit of barbaric vandalism, all traces of their religious and cultural life from their country, although Islamic culture had greatly enriched their own lives. They succeeded, however, in exiling Islam from the country where it had showered its innumerable blessings.

One consequence of this vandalism was that western renaissance was delayed by many centuries, and when it did come at last, it started in the wrong way, of mistaken conceptions about human life and destiny. As a result, Europe itself and the whole world of which it had become the intellectual leader became plunged in godlessness, moral anarchy and the pursuit of material desires and comforts. Europe had received no real light and no true guidance from religion. It was led by a few superstitions, prejudices and certain commentaries and

Interpretations of Christian scholars. The latter had compiled a whole world geography and an ecclesiastical world history which clashed with scientific discoveries and the latest advances in knowledge. A stable and virtuous civilization can be built only on a correct conception of God, His attributes, the necessity of divine revelation and its role in ordering human affairs and a view of life which shows man his right place in the total scheme of life. These things were totally strange to the European mind and a perverted Christianity could hardly offer any guidance in the matter. It was concerned only with the preservation of the spiritual and temporal power of the Church, and it insisted on the absolute veracity of the geographical and physical references in the scriptures. Europe, in short, had never had the opportunity to understand and realise what a real religion could be like. If it had known real religion, the conflict between science and religion could have been easily avoided with all its evil consequences. So long as Islam was dominant in Spain, there was still a chance for Europe to realise the value of religion as a society-shaping power. But having missed it, through its blindness and prejudice, Europe had no alternative but to fall back on Christianity as the sole representative of religion, and Christianity in the form in which it then existed gave totally false idea of religion. It made no distinction between the eternal values of life and the readjustments needed in social affairs owing to the change of circumstances. The standard-bearers of Christianity stood in the way of every intellectual advance and scientific progress, because they stuck to the old commentaries of the Gospels. They even went to the length of inflicting severe punishments upon the new scientists and philosophers who repudiated old notions such as the movement of the sun around the earth and the flatness of the earth. In consequence of their intellectual obscurantism and terrorism, men of light and learning all over Europe rebelled against religion and started their scientific investigations and philosophical speculation in complete indifference, nay, blind opposition, to all religion and morality.

This wrong start in the field of knowledge produced many undesirable consequences. It made the progress of western enlightenment aimless. European sciences lost all sense of direction. They missed the higher and more ultimate realities of knowledge. The European mind, no doubt, discovered innumerable new facts and was able to bring forward an imposing array of scientific truths into a coherent system such as could offer guidance to humanity in search of righteous living.

Another evil aspect of this mutual antagonism between religion and the new knowledge was that the new learning, having freed itself from the guidance and discipline of religion, was also cut off from all moral values and ethical standards.

The new sciences achieved victory after victory in the field of knowledge, but they left humanity in a deeper morass of moral degeneration than they found him. The increase of knowledge meant an increase of power in the hands of individuals and communities, but there was nothing in the life of the new civilization which could control the fast-increasing powers of human beings over Nature. Man became a giant of mental powers and physical resources, but in his passions and emotions he remained as ever a child and, in his inclinations, and predilections he became a follower of the devil. He has obtained control over the air, the steam and electricity, he has acquired command of the Innumerable forces of Nature, but he remains ignorant of and indifferent to the forces of virtue and righteousness and the objectives of a good, healthy and balanced life, for these things can come only from a particular type of religious training which is anathema to the modern mind. Man is wasting his powers and resources either over trivial objects which are useful to humanity only within very narrow limits or in destructive savageries fatal to his own life and to the civilization which he has built. National selfishness dominates the scene in Europe leading to national and class conflicts which destroy the lives and happiness of millions of human beings. Not content with this, Europe and America are now planning for a global war in which atom bomb will mercilessly destroy and annihilate all traces of human life and culture.

All the scientific discoveries of Europe and all stupendous knowledge will prove useless without the guidance of religion. There is much that is useful in this knowledge for partial and one-sided objectives and within narrow field of life, but, on the whole, it does not give us the governing principles of life, on which a healthy corporate existence may be built. Europe has solved many complex questions and answered many difficult enquiries about processes of the external physical universe, but the complex problems of its own life still defy solution and become every day more complex, more tangled, and more difficult of solution. There is now only one way for the salvation of the western world and that is to acknowledge its moral and intellectual bankruptcy as far as the ultimate issues of life and the guiding principles of social and corporate existence are concerned, and to turn to religion and prophetic revelation for the solution of its social and spiritual difficulties. Only a religion which gives the western nations the real objectives of life and a correct conception of God, His attributes and His methods, which fills the western mind with the love and fear of the Divine Being, which enlightens and awakens its soul without weakening its intellect, which creates a powerful condition and a strong faith in the existence of a future life wherein man will have to render his accounts for all his overt and covert deeds and which provides him with the example of a living prophetic personality whose life and works have been fully recorded by historians with full details and whose actions furnish guidance in every field of life, be it social, political, private or public, can save European civilization from imminent collapse. A religion of this kind will not be religion. In the western sense of the word, it will be a complete social order resting on certain moral principles whose actual working has been exemplified in the lives of millions of human beings belonging to different periods of history and in conformity with which the administration and governments of many countries and empires have been run. This religion will be free from the monasticism of Christianity, the materialism of the modern West, the yogic beliefs and practices of ancient India, the luxurious living of the Persians, the softness and aesthetic excesses of the Greeks and the rough harshness of the Stoic philosophy. It should teach neither unqualified and absolute non-violence nor psychological and physical violence. It should repudiate nationalism and stress the essential unity of all nations, races and classes. It should make human beings less selfish and free them from the domination of desires. In short, it should provide a complete antidote to the many evils from which mankind is suffering and harness the energies of man to the constructive tasks of civilization.

This kind of teaching with all the qualifications enumerated above is still extant in the contents of the holy Quran which is the only religious book free from human interpolations and existing in all its pristine purity. It is a book which can still infuse new life in the nations of the world and whose inexhaustible intellectual wealth can easily solve the problems with which all the modern world finds itself confronted. It is a Book which with its profundity of thought is easily accessible to the average human understanding and does not require laboured interpretations to make itself intelligible to the common man.

Muhammad is the only divine Prophet whose life and teachings are still applicable to human problems in the vastly changed conditions of modern life. in the life of the Arabian Prophet the rich as well as the poor, the powerful as well as the weak, the ruler as well as the trader, the husband as well as the father, the treaty-maker as well as the sovereign at war with an enemy country, the young as well as the old can find practical guidance. He is the only one among the whole line of prophets whose life, both public and private, in all its multifarious details has been recorded by reliable observers with strict historical veracity. Everyone can profit by his life and example.

In the laws enunciated by the holy Prophet, one can find principles of life and norms of conduct on the basis of which a healthy civilization and an equitable social order can be built, and human faculties may be provided with opportunities of fullest development.

This life-giving force is within easy reach of the western nations but it will amount to an admission of failure if they turn to it and this is precisely what stands in the way of their taking the right path. The people who are at the helm of western affairs will rather see nations destroyed, countries devastated, and the entire humanity plunged in distress rather than make the damaging admission and declare their own bankruptcy. They go on making one experiment after another without any success, they run from one quack to another, but their social and moral diseases keep steadily increasing. A false sense of prestige and a false pride in their scientific and material progress prevents them from turning to the unlettered Prophet, who alone offers the hope of salvation to a diseased and distressed humanity. The result of this self-conceit is that generations after generations of mankind face death and destruction and humanity itself is confronted with a dire threat to its life and existence.

The Asiatic nations which are following in the foot- steps of the European nations are faced with an even darker future. They lack the spiritual power which alone can save human beings from the slavery of desire and enable them to resist temptations. The great teachings of the ancient prophets which once had cast their healthy and beneficial influence on the peoples of the East have become a spent force owing to studied negligence on the part of these peoples and they have been pervert- ed out of shape by the hair-splitting discussions of scholars and the logic-chopping habits of the philosophers. On the other hand, the nations of the East lack the sense of national solidarity and the consciousness of citizenship possessed by the nations of the West with the result that they cannot rise above petty selfish ends and are suffering from moral and social weaknesses of a destructive character which are undermining their social fabric. With this moral backwardness, they have now assumed the responsibilities of governments in their own countries, as a result of world conditions. In con- sequence, innumerable social and moral evils have come to the surface and social vices like bribery, corruption and partisanship which operated in a restricted sphere have assumed enormous proportions.

However, these evils are not the real diseases from which society is suffering. They are only symptoms of a far greater and deeper disease, that is, excessive love and worship of life. When individuals and nations are gripped by this disease, states and empires disintegrate, nations are enslaved and subjugated, brother plots against brother, treachery, deceit and cruelty become the order of the day. It is not easy to cure them of these diseases. Education and enlightenment are not of much avail in the task of eradicating them.

There is only one way to fight this cancer: it is to Inspire men with a sincere faith in God and in the accountability of man and to create in men's minds the fear and hope of a future life. No human philosophy, no mere extension of knowledge can create this revolutionary faith. It is only the great prophets of God and their sincere followers who can achieve this miracle and Inspire men with the faith and vision of a new life.

Every now and then the world must turn to them for acquiring this power of faith, for they are the only custodians of this inexhaustible treasure. No doubt nations have produced their own philosophers, poets, scholars, soldiers, statesmen and heroes, and their history does not lack examples of great selflessness, shining sincerity and super-human sacrifices. There are noble traditions of loyalty, patriotism and love of liberty. These must be preserved and perpetuated by the governments and peoples concerned for they are a precious heritage. But they are patently insufficient as a guiding and ennobling force in the complexities of man's collective life and the shaping of human destinies; philosophical profundities and scholarly hair-splitting cannot lead us out of our present difficulties. It is only the teachings of the Arabian Prophet which rescued humanity thirteen hundred years ago out of the morass of social, moral and spiritual degradation and brought mankind to the path of righteousness that can still save us from the dangers which threaten us with annihilation. These teachings have been preserved intact by his followers and are still capable of giving us the right lead.

Asia is more fortunate in that the teachings of the Prophet of Islam are easier of access to it and the peoples of this continent can receive much more easily the guidance which they contain in such abundant measure. All nations can draw upon this source of strength and social health for it is not the monopoly of any particular race or nationality. Just as in the past the Seljuks and then the Ottoman Turks assumed the leadership of the Muslim world and replaced the Arabs as the champions of Islam, so it is equally open to any modern nation to adopt the teachings of the Prophet and become the spear- head of a new movement and the spiritual leader of man- kind in place of the present-day Muslims who seem to have lost the spirit of those teachings.

If any of your children or those whom you hold dear suffers from illness or disease you run to every doctor or physician and do not confine your efforts to any particular system of medicine. You have an open-mind and examine with absolute impartiality the claims of every alternative method of treatment. The same impartiality and open-mindedness should be extended to rival theories of life and competing socio-religious orders by those who are presiding over the destinies of an ailing civilization or guiding the affairs of particular nations which suffer from social and moral weakness of a dangerous nature. Surely the responsibilities of national and international leaders are much greater than those of the people who have to look after diseased and sick men. If the latter can rise above their personal likes and dislikes in order to save the life of their dear ones, those at the helm of affairs of ailing peoples and nations should be much more open-minded and catholic in the search for social cures with a view to bringing salvation, peace and stability to their peoples. The twentieth century can say to the nations of the world what the holy Quran said to the peoples of the sixth century: -

> "Light and guidance has come to you from God. Those who desire to earn the pleasure of God are shown the way of peace and safety by the Quran and such people are taken out by God from darkness into light and led to the right path."[16]

---

[16] Q. V: 15-16

To the students receiving a modern education

Speech delivered before a largely attended meeting of students belonging to India, Pakistan and to Arab Countries, held at the Islamic Centre, London in October 1964. It has been rendered into English by Mohiuddin Ahmad.

5

A Prediction

I am neither a seer, nor saint nor prophet, nor I claim to be a divinator, but today I would like to make a prediction: AND THIS PREDICTION is that many amongst, you would wield the reins of governments or hold responsible positions of rank and authority in your own countries. You are at present pursuing your education here but these offices are awaiting your return to your homes. I can foresee your bright prospects from your shining countenance. There was a time when it was necessary to possess personal valour and learn the art of warfare- the trade of the kings to rule over a country. Conquerors of lands and nations like Alexander, Chenghiz and Halaku chained victory to their cars at the point of sword. But an appeal to the sword is no longer necessary to hold the sceptre of authority. Now the key of knowledge opens the way to leadership and guarantees governance of a country. The path of democracy be taken by every civilized country as also the Islamic lands and the problems they have to face today clearly indicate that only those will preside over the destinies of their countries who are adept in various branches of western learning and have gained mastery over at least one of its languages. The modern democratic set up provides you with the opportunities and means to take the reins of government in your hands. It is for these reasons that I hope that one day you would be at the helm of authority in your countries. This would, in other words, afford you an opportunity to serve your country and the people. But this also means a crucial test of your abilities for the future of these lands will then depend on the course you would decide to adopt.

World of Islam

The countries you come from and to which you shall have to return after completing your education are Muslim countries. They have been Muslim for a long time and so shall they remain in future also. They have acquired the wealth of Islam after undergoing immense sacrifices and therefore they hold it dear to their heart. It is a valuable possession they cherish most. The vast majority of the population in these countries, some of which are even larger in area and population than some of the most populous countries of Europe, is Muslim. In natural resources too they are so rich that even the West has to depend on them for moving the wheels of its industry. Modern science and technology owe much of their progress to these very resources. No country in the world has, in truth, been endowed with the wealth possessed by these countries.

In a similar way, the people living in these lands possess sterling human qualities; they are pulsating with the vigour of life and moral strength. They have driven and agility, sacrificing zeal and noble mindedness and devotion and steadfastness-qualities not to be found in any other nation of the world.

Those who have traversed the world and have experience of the different lands and peoples acknowledge the fact that no other nation has the qualities possessed by these Muslims. Imbued with the vital spark of life, they can still sacrifice their life for a righteous cause. If they could find a correct leadership, they can still become a great power of the world. Other nations lack their sincerity, large-heartedness, devotion and warmth of feeling but it is also a fact, albeit much to be regretted, that these qualities of head and heart are being wasted for a considerable time. The leadership of these countries is completely oblivious to the worth of its people: it has neither the capacity nor the will to channelise the energies of its people for the betterment of these nation.

If I were asked to name the greatest problem facing the world of Islam today, I would unhesitatingly declare that it consists of the lack of intellectual rapport between the leaders and the masses of these countries which has created a mental cleavage and class struggle and given rise to a shattering unrest. The Muslim masses adhere to Islam, they want to live and die for it, they do not understand any language other than the language of faith, nothing has a greater charm for them than God and His Apostle, Hereafter and the Heaven, fighting for the cause of religion and dying for it, submitting to the Will of God and earning His pleasure. Nor can anything except a call for the defence of their faith warm their blood and fan the flame of frenzied fervour in them. This was the cry which stirred the embers of sacrificing zeal among the people of Algeria, whose sufferings for their cause are unsurpassed by those undergone by any other people of the world. The tide of liberation movements let loose in every Islamic country was inspired by this very religious zeal. The Muslims of these countries love and revere the law contained in their Scripture and sincerely believe it to be superior to all man-made laws. They love their culture and the way of life; they want to see these flourish- Ing in their lands; they desire the commandments of God to be enforced in their lives; for, they have no affection, no fancy for anything except these.

A Great Tragedy

But, unfortunately, the coterie gaining a hold upon these countries and claiming to be their guide and philosopher, has had its education and training in an atmosphere entirely different from that obtaining in their own lands. Its mental outlook and way of looking at things has been cast in an entirely different mould. It has had its education and training in the cities in which you are pursuing your studies at present. It has been made to believe by their teachers that the era of Islam has now come to an end. It has been dinned into their ears that Islam, on making its debut, had undoubtedly served a useful purpose by leading humanity on the path of civilization and enlightenment, but now it has hardly anything to offer to the civilized and progressive societies. Now it does not simply fit in with the changed circum- stances. The people living in these countries are still zealous believers, who can still produce Muhammad Bin Qasim, Tariq-ibn-Ziyad, Musa Bin Nasir and Muhammad the Conqueror. But how unfortunate it is that the leaders presiding over their destinies have lost faith in Islam; they have given it up as a lost case; they have abandoned all hopes in its future and have not the least interest in it! Verily, they had come to Europe to learn its arts and sciences and to master the technology and industry of the West so as to put these to the service of Islam!

A New Suez Canal

They had come to Europe to dig a New Suez Canal -a canal which could act as a channel for exchanging the goods and ideas between the East and the West on the basis of parity and equality. Such a channel could have served to transmit the wealth of faith and virtuous living to the West and harmless wherewithal of material progress and development to the East. But, alas, the persons who could have fulfilled this noble task were content with remaining mere imitators of the West. Their achievements are devoid of all intelligence and originality, courage and novelty. Instead of being exemplars they have proved themselves to be the poll-parrots of the West. Iqbal had truly said:

"Those who could have led the world of their Age,

The dullards are, alas, mimics of the times' craze."

My dear friends, you have not come to Europe to be cast in any mould like a molten wax. You have come here to build a brave new world-a world that can be built only by the sons and followers of Ibrahim. This world can now be reconstructed only by those very virtuous hands which had erected the edifice of Haram, the first House of God, on this earth. The world is calling you today in anguish:

"Rise, O Architect of Haram, rise to reconstruct the world anew."

The Observed of all Observers

You have definitely not come to Europe to walk in the shoes of the West on going back to your homes. The East requires such sagacious and courageous souls who can point out the blunders made by the West and rise above its outlook and attitudes, and its way of life. They should be able to challenge the West in the words of Ibrahim:

"We have done with you. And there hath arisen between us and you hostility and hate forever until you believe in Allah only."

(*Al-Mumtahanah*: 4)

The East does not need those men who always stand behind the West nodding their heads in approval of whatever it does. It now needs such daring and bold young men who can fearlessly set their face against the West.

Those who bend their necks before the West but crush the East under an iron heel are not worth their salt. The present leadership of Turkey, Indonesia, Egypt and other Muslim countries has not been able to show any originality or worth. You have to go a long, long way ahead of them. They have jettisoned everything they had at the altar of West but what they got in return was insignificant as com- pared to the wealth thrown overboard by them.

Not Scientists and Engineers Alone

My friends, you ought to know that those who have sent you here for higher studies do not want you merely to become scientists, technicians, engineers and artists or to gain some knowledge of a European language. If you become merely these, you would not be able to render any useful service to your country the service which it needs most. You ought to become a masters in these branches of learning. If you are studying, say Law, then you should devote yourself assiduously to learn all about different legal systems including Islamic jurisprudence in order to establish the superiority of the laws of Shariah over other man-made laws. You should be able to understand and tell your people how out of shape Europe has become. Bent with age, it is likely to fall away any moment like a yellow leaf!

If you go back from here to tell your people that the West is all goodness and virtue, you would be telling a lie and deceiving your people. You ought to be able to tell your people the praiseworthy qualities of the West, the secret of its strength and the things that can profitable be borrowed from it; but, at the same time, you should also let your people know the weaknesses and the ailments from which Europe is suffering and which have sapped its moral strength and vitality. You ought to be able to distinguish the things that can be emulated from those which have to be avoided, for the latter have nothing to do with economic prosperity and material power of the western nations.

You can still Do a Lot

Had I told these to the people in Delhi, Karachi, Cairo or any other capital of the eastern countries or their leaders who have already chosen a way of life for them, these would not have had the desired effect. The mental attitudes and intellectual moulds are cast here, in these cities, which start manifesting themselves in the eastern countries. It is, therefore, the right place and the right time to warn you, for, you have to wield the reins of governments in your countries, guide and lead your people. You have to build your nations. Therefore, if you could realise right now the true worth and capabilities of your people, learn to appreciate their values of life and begin to pin your faith in the worth and inner strength of Islam, then, believe me, you would have learnt everything.

A Call for Action

The countries that are to be committed to your care are quite vast and populous lands. Few countries in the world have such a great manpower at their disposal. You should carefully assess the human and natural resources of your countries, draw up your plans for their development and take full advantage of your knowledge to achieve your ends. You should set an example of selfless service to your people and noble devotion to your cause. If you could do that and guide your people on the path of Islam, you would be able to carve out for you a place of lasting fame infinitely superior to that enjoyed by any other leader in the East. It would be a place not accorded by history to Mustafa Kamal Ata Turk or Gamal Abdul Nasir, Ben Bella or Ahmad Soekarno.

Such a place of loving adoration and confidence of the people can be had only by selfless sacrifice for the regeneration of the Millat and by proclaiming the message of God to the world. Providence has reserved this place for the chosen few alone. But if you could manage to make the grade you would save these countries from the intellectual unrest, moral confusion and class struggle which have been unnecessarily fomented by their national leaders. The strife going on in the East is totally against the values and traditions and national characteristics of these nations.

A Quest for the Self

You ought to be aware of your own abilities and capabilities of your own nations; the potentialities and the reservoirs of strength lying hidden in your people, which can open the way for you to a great and lasting achievement. You have to discover your own selves and the new world you have to build for your people.

You may or may not understand what I say, but do try to understand your own selves.

Responsibilities of Muslim Young men proceeding to the West

The article written for Islamic Centre, Geneva, was published in Al-Muslimoon, Cairo, in its 1961 issue. Translated into English by Dr. M. Asif Kidwai.

6

FRIENDS!

From across the oceans, I send you my earnest greetings and best wishes. These are indicative of my deep sincerity and hearty Islamic feeling. I believe your voyage to Europe or America or your stay at any of the educational, cultural or industrial centres of the West is not a chance occurrence or an impulsive act that takes place without conscious decision or intention. Nor is it a calamity which may call for sympathy and consolation.

In my view, whether your voyage is for a few days or in the nature of permanent migration and whatever its aims and objectives may be, it is, after all, an opportunity and a favour conferred by God.

This voyage is a blessing for you individually as well as for the modern social environment which is prevailing all over the world. By it, I mean the western social system which includes both the Soviet Union and United States. This is an opportunity that will lead to the promotion and strengthening your faith in Islam, in the holy Quran and in the call of the sacred Apostles and the teachings of the Prophet Mohammad (Peace and Blessings of Allah be on him); for, the Divine Apostleship and message of the holy Prophet and his

Inspired teachings that are eternal are even today wholly capable of becoming popular and exercising an everlasting influence in the world.

You are now under the full glare of the new learning of West which, after a long spell of social and intellectual inertia and stagnation of Europe, brought about a revolution in the realm of its thought and gave it a new lease of life.

Western Concept of Life

The most important thing from your point of view is that the champions of the modern civilization claim that civilised society can also come into being away from spiritual convictions, religious beliefs, moral values and Apostolic teachings; and not only that, they assert that it should be so and its foundations should rest on knowledge and science, trade and industry, political and economic stability, nationalism and patriotism and legal and constitutional covenants and arrangements. They, further, hold that social progress and advancement is related wholly to the modern means and machines which are the products of their physical sciences.

The successes of the society and the welfare of mankind signify that man should conquer the world and the forces of nature for the satisfaction of his carnal appetites. In material sciences alone lies his salvation. The failure of man in the past was due simply to the fact that the channels for the exchange of ideas were blocked and the world was divided into different parts.

The West tried to propagate this view with the enthusiasm of a fanatic. Its slogans were as: There is no God, no Religion, no Unseen, no Spirit and no Futurity. According to it the Shariat and its spiritual structure are mere superstition. The real ingredients of life are perception, experience, pleasure, gain, nationalism, freedom, democracy and communism.

Harmful Effects

The protagonists as well as critics of this viewpoint appeared on the stage of the world armed with their ideas and ideals and they effected an intellectual diversion of the West. Consequently, various schools of thoughts came to flourish whose influence can be seen today in the entire range of learning and literatures. The modern western society has profited from all of them and accepted their influence in a greater or lesser degree. It has made materialism its hall mark.

The West is now in a position to enforce the ideas and principles in which it believes freely and openly. It is a unique event of history. Owing to its phenomenal power and resources the West has been able to play its role most successfully. Its achievement is unparalleled in the history of World leadership. Even more culturally and intellectually gifted nations had not been able to establish such a complete and universal ascendancy.

When Europe embarked on its course of progress and expansion, there was no power in the world that could challenge it or impede its advance. The Church had capitulated before the mental and political revolt of the Christendom long ago. The Islamic East yielded to its political and intellectual might in the 19th Century and the whole world went on submitting to it quietly and quickly.

Incidentally, Europe got the opportunity to present its capabilities in the material form and its materialistic creed was received everywhere willingly and enthusiastically. But the whole show came to a tragic end. It proved to be a colossal failure. As a result of it, there is both inner and outer discord and confusion; individuals, classes and communities are at loggerheads with each other, and the horizon is darkened with the clouds of war. The World is presenting the spectacle of a powder-keg which is ready to explode at any moment. Woeful cries are being raised at the expectation of the disastrous end of humanity. Self-confidence, peace and emotional equipoise are things of the past. Man is haunted with fear. His soul is restless. He is troubled about the future. A perpetual feeling of anxiety is felt everywhere; moral turmoil is complete, and the spiritual vacuum is becoming more fearful every day. There is an incurable sense of despondency and frustration. On all sides, there is nothing but distress, misery, and bitterness.

The story of the wretchedness and infelicity of the western civilization is such that it deserves to be told again and again. It is the most important episode in the history of human species for in the East there are still people who believe in its purity and innocence and look upon it with respect and envy. They are confident that a civilization like it can never perish or become insolvent. They pay regard to it with religious reverence.

Weaknesses of the Materialistic System

You live in the midst of this civilization and feel its scorching heat. You observe its anguish and uneasiness and see evidence of its decay and degeneration in all places. You notice its intrinsic traits in the moral dis- position of its political leaders, in the disregard of human sentiments, in the neglect of ethical values and in the high incidence of crime and other grave moral offences. You see it unveiled in the conduct and philosophy of the leaders of thought and politics who are utterly incapable of appreciating the message of humanity and carrying it to others and wholly insensitive to the call of the spirit that can breathe a new life into the society, lead the community towards its high destination and bring about harmony and integration. This civilization, at the height of its victory, is suffering from the crisis of confidence.

This state of affairs should be sufficient to convince you that a society which is not based on faith is destined to an evil fate. It is another matter that it manages to prolong its life a little more, but it is bound to come to a tragic end.

In fact, it is the path of belief and faith and the message and the life-example of the Divine Apostles that uplift the character of both individuals and communities, and illumine it with the light of spiritual feeling. They impart the spirit of faith and courage independently of academies and educational institutions and means of propaganda and mass communication. Faith cures the hearts of greed, hypocrisy, boastfulness and ostentation, and pro- motes life and vitality and gives rise to belief in the Here- after, sincerity and selflessness. It convinces one of the transitoriness of the world, strengthens faith in God whom no human eye has seen nor mind can comprehend and arouses in man the sentiments of laying down one's life for His sake. History still remembers the deeds of these men of faith and conviction. Had such events not taken place so repeatedly the world would perhaps have repudiated them without hesitation. This is the segment of humanity which has preserved the vanishing stock of civilization, rescued the society again and again from the depths of waywardness and pulled the boat of mankind out of the whirlwind of death in the nick of time. These high-souled men have always saved the moral values and higher human concepts from destruction. In all their endeavours they have been guided by earnestness and solicitude for the deliverance of mankind.

Universal Distinctiveness of Islam

It is an incontrovertible fact that the ancient faiths which have come to the aid of mankind and furnished it with right guidance at the hour of its need, and whose glorious contribution to human upliftment is unforgettable have lost their vitality owing to the vicissitudes of time. They are a spent force today and cannot be depended upon to repel onslaught of materialism in the modern age. Even the upholders of these religions have lost faith in them. They are not suited to the exigencies of the present days and religious fervour and the spirit of endeavour also is lacking in them. They are as powerless as a paralysed limb so far as meeting the menace of the modern civilization is concerned. Most of them have already laid down their arms before the Western civilization and accepted that there is no escape from materialism which is the last stage in the evolution of human civilization.

But at this critical juncture there is a religion which is safe and unpolluted. It is both living and life giving, true and realistic, pure and free from all faults and weaknesses. Its followers know that they are responsible for the superintendence of the world, the survival of civilization and the close examination of the good and evil propensities of mankind. They will have to render account of the way they discharge their duty.

This faith is distinguished from other faiths in four respects: -

1. It possesses the Great Book which vibrates with life and is effulgent with human felicity. It provides a sound leadership to mankind and contains knowledge which is both profound and unbounded. For mind and intellect, it is an ever- lasting source of joy and hopefulness, a spring- head that never dries up. Its ever-flowing stream does, in no case, get isolated from life. It

has wrought a mighty revolution in the lives of men and can do it again any day. It can once more infuse a new life into leadership and cause a tumult in its waves.

2. Similarly the record of the sayings and doings of the holy Prophet, his life-account, is a fragrant legacy which is extremely beautiful as well as incandescent. It makes the most shining page of the story of human advancement which can be recreated by reminding mankind of its true station. The reading of it restores the confidence of man in himself and revives in him the awareness of his nobility. The picture it presents Is so exquisitely charming that anyone whose aesthetic sense has not deserted him and in whom the feeling of perfection is present cannot fail to be aroused and inspired by it. He will be seized with the ambition to attain the heights by emulating the Prophet's example that may endue his life with sublimity, peace, and magnanimity. It unties the knots of intellect and unravels the hidden mysteries. This wonderful portrait of lofty virtues and splendid accomplishments is present to this day in its pristine glory and the alteration of circumstances, and the passage of time have done nothing to rob it of its purity or radiance.

The preserved treasure of the Islamic Shariat is present, without any distortion or amendment, as it was left behind by the bringer of the Shariat, the Prophet himself.

The Shariat is the completest and the most perfect jurisprudential system in the world. It denotes an admirable blending of the ancient with the modern and can serve the needs of all ages and climes. It is also well established for the future. It possesses such wise and sound foundations that the edifice of a healthy society or civilization can always be built on them.

4. The adherents of Islam are characterised by religious fervour and enthusiasm which no other community can boast of. In spite of all their lethargy, listlessness and neglect of faith the spark of Islam is still hidden in their hearts. They are ready to the call of an earnest preacher and to make the supreme sacrifice in the path of Allah. This is the charming aspect of belief and vitality of which the Western nations are totally devoid today. Anyone who has the occasion to work in any community for religious revival and reform will have no difficulty in confirming it.

Responsibility of the Educated Youth

Muslim young men who are living in Europe or America or studying there are a part of the great Islamic Millat. They are the members of the same international family and the inheritors of the same legacy. By 'family' we do not mean what the common people associate with blood ties, nor does legacy signify what the Orientalists and other ignorant scholars seek to suggest. They furnish the proof of their lack of knowledge by writing books on what, they are so fond of calling 'The Legacy of Islam'. Here we mean the brotherhood of the deep-hearted- ed servants of the Lord who may have attained a place of distinction by striving their level best in the path of faith and learning.

Reading Afresh of Islamics

Learned Young Men!

You should undertake a fresh study of Islam and examine it in the light of the distinguishing features I have briefly mentioned above. You should try to understand Islam in a new way and along the modern lines, seriously and sincerely. You ought to study the Quran not with the aid of written commentaries but with the depths of your mind and heart. Make use of your perspicacity and sound judgement while learning it. You should read it as if it was not an old scripture but the one that has been sent down for the current age, or, rather, that it is being revealed to you directly. You ought to spend your precious time on the study of the life of the Prophet and his Traditions and try to forge a living contact with him. This contact should be based on study, love, devotion, and dedication.

Representatives of Islam

Next, it is your duty to function as the true representatives of Islam in the West. You should boldly present the tenets of your faith, show a correct image of it, and safeguard its teachings, commands, and practices. You are the representatives of a religion which is the Best of Religions and ideally suited for the modern times. Your faith needs you.

Set a Good Example

You ought to present a good image of Islam before your friends and other young men who feel shy of being known as Muslims. You have to set a good example for the young men coming from Muslim countries or receiving education at Arab institutions who refrain from giving expression to Islam. For it there is definitely the promise of a permanent reward. You can attract your friends, teachers, and neighbours by leading a truly Islamic life of piety and truthfulness, prayer and remembrance, contentment and serenity and joy and virility. History tells that Islam has drawn to itself countless intellectuals in this way and conquered whole nations and communities without shedding a drop of blood.

May be, you are on the rolls of a University or working in a factory or in an office. Your rank may be high or low but your existence, by virtue of your creed and message, is most exalted. You owe certain duties to your teachers from whom you may have learnt anything, and Islam attaches the greatest importance to rendering to everyone what may be his due. They need you in order to understand Islam properly. You hold the position of a guide and mentor with regard to them.

Unique Opportunity:

Realise your worth and value in these circumstances: understand your responsibility and fulfil your duty. I say to you, once again, that your stay in Europe or America is a unique opportunity from which you should derive the fullest advantage. Through it you can also pave the way for the resurgence of Islam and the welfare of humanity. Your presence in these lands will be a source of strength to your faith; it will lead to the placing of trust and reliance on it and new avenues for the progress of Islam will open up as a result of it.

You are at a place where the blessing of Islam has been non-existent for a long time. The way of life that is followed there is inimical to the Divine Message and the fundamentals of Apostleship. It is opposed to moral values and spiritual standards.

Your presence can be instrumental in filling this awful void.

www.ingramcontent.com/pod-product-compliance
Ingram Content Group UK Ltd.
Pitfield, Milton Keynes, MK11 3LW, UK
UKHW021359190726
13845UKWH00028B/770

9 789394 770775